Emmanuelle Courrèges

The Fashion Continent

AFRICA

Flammarion

CONTENTS

Page 1:
Final runway show of Ituen Basi's "Dear George" collection, Arise Fashion Week, Lagos, Nigeria, April 21, 2019.
© Bennett Raglin/Getty Images.

Pages 2–3:
Maison ART/C (brand created by Artsi Ifrach), "Beautiful Sadness" collection, chosen to represent Morocco at the Hub of Africa Fashion Week, Addis-Ababa, Ethiopia, October 2018.
© Artsimous (Artsi Ifrach and Mous Lamrabat).

Pages 4–5:
Post-Imperial (brand created by Niyi Okuboyejo), "Jollof" collection, fall 2020.
© Joshua Kissi.

Page 6:
Trevor Stuurman, portrait of Nike Okundaye, artist and founder of the Nike Art Gallery in Lagos, Nigeria, April 23, 2019.
© Trevor Stuurman.

Page 7:
Daily Paper (brand created by Hussein Suleiman, Jefferson Osei, and Abderrahmane Trabsini), look from the fall-winter 2019 collection, modeled by Patrice Kouadio.
© Mous Lamrabat.

Page 8:
Adama Paris (brand created by Adama Ndiaye) runway show at Black Fashion Week in Paris, France, October 5, 2012.
© Photo12/ABC/Ammar Abd Rabbo.

Page 9:
Abdel El Tayeb, skirt, plastron top, and headdress from the "Ma Nation Porte Ton Nom (Hommage à Mon Père) [My Nation Bears Your Name (Tribute to My Father)]" collection, modeled by Aminata Mbengue and Chad Yvan. Photograph published in Dazed magazine (no. 272, June 2021). Styling: Marquet K. Lee. Hair: Yann Turchi. Makeup: Aurore Gibrien.
© Casper Kofi.

Pages 10–11:
Karim Adduchi runway show, "She Knows Why the Caged Bird Sings" collection, spring-summer 2015.
Courtesy Karim Adduchi.

Page 12:
Malick Welli, Thioro and Nara, from the "Duet" series, 2017.
Courtesy of Galerie Clémentine de la Féronnière.

Page 13:
Viviers (brand created by Lezanne Viviers), looks from the "Unfold" collection, fall-winter 2019, modeled by Caleb Nkosi and Rhulani Kubayi. Hair: Studio Lennie. Makeup: Caroline Greef.
© Nico Krijno.

Page 14:
Duro Olowu, coat, dresses, and scarves from the fall-winter 2019 collection.
© Luís Montero.

Facing page:
Lukhanyo Mdingi, jacket, sweaters, and pants from the fall-winter 2019 collection, modeled by Roldy Kaya and Pivot Aurel Sentore.
© Jarred Figgins.

PREFACE

To write about African fashion in the fifty-four countries that comprise the continent is an impossible task. Africa's myriad cultures, the number of talented designers and photographers that make it stand out today on the local and international fashion scenes, and the creative energy of the African diasporas in Europe, Brazil, and the United States cannot be contained in a single work. For this reason, I have chosen in this book to focus more on what is happening within the African continent than outside of it, barring a few noteworthy exceptions.

Africa: The Fashion Continent is not a history of African fashion. Rather, it reflects the new aesthetics taking form and, led by the designers shaping them, offers an interpretation of the underlying inspiration. The book is an insightful snapshot of a generation of artists who, in many ways, are revolutionizing the world's perception of Africa.

The African continent shaped who I am. I spent the first eighteen years of my life there, living between Cameroon, Senegal, and Ivory Coast. Then, as a young journalist working for a pan-African press group, I covered African fashion weeks and festivals focused on textiles and raw materials produced on the continent. Since starting out twenty years ago, I have continued to meet with and listen to the protagonists driving African fashion, affirming its vitality in international magazines like *ELLE* and *Vogue Italia.*

Two people played a particularly important role in cultivating my awareness of this sector: the sociologist Aminata Dramane Traoré, Mali's former minister of culture; and the Malian designer Chris Seydou. I was incredibly privileged to come of age alongside these two exceptional individuals, to whom this book is dedicated. As an adolescent, I saw Aminata Traoré wear clothes "made in Africa," modern and traditional garments accessorized with creations by young African designers. An impassioned advocate of fashion's economic and cultural potential, Aminata insisted on the importance of "buying local," on the added value of cotton transformed in cotton-producing countries by talented designers, and on the necessity of cultivating renewed appreciation for skills and know-how. Although these ideas have since become fashionable, in the 1980s Aminata was one of the rare individuals who not only shared this message, but also believed in and embodied it.

Chris Seydou, considered to be the pioneer of contemporary African fashion, was also a family friend. Chris was the first designer to create a modern wardrobe using *bogolan* cloth; up to that point, the fabric had been excluded from the sphere of fashion due to its "traditional" aspect. In a way, his work gave form to Aminata's thinking. They were also very close friends. There in Africa, witness to two of the continent's most powerful voices who shaped my conception and my political consciousness of clothing, I wove an inextricable link to African fashion.

In the West, African fashion has long been the victim of preconceived ideas. Reduced to obsolete images, it has struggled (and still struggles) to be respected. Disregarded by the mainstream media—with the notable exception of *Vogue Italia*—its chief representatives have rarely been given coverage. Above all, African fashion, when it is not invisible, remains incomprehensible for many.

I conceived this book as a response to everyone I have ever heard claim that there is nothing "African" about contemporary African fashion. At a time when many talented African designers are gradually making their mark on an international scale, and as the spotlight shines more intensely on this "fashion continent," I saw the need to provide some keys to understanding it, by allowing those who embody African fashion to have their say— or at least a few of them. This book is a tribute to them; it captures a moment in History, and presents a creative, engaged generation that is changing fashion as we know it.

EMMANUELLE COURRÈGES

Maxhosa Africa (brand created by Laduma Ngxokolo), coat, sweater, and dress from the "Evolution of Maxhosa" collection, fall 2018, backstage at Fashion Week during the African Fashion International in Cape Town, South Africa, March 2018.
© Per-Anders Pettersson/Getty Images.

INTRODUCTION

frican fashion has never received as much attention as it has in recent years. Previously absent from international fashion circles, it blazed its way into the official fashion week schedules in Paris, Milan, and New York. Majestic kente cloth by Cameroonian Imane Ayissi; *aso-oke* fabric woven in effusive rainbow colors by Nigerian Kenneth Ize; boldly poetic and politicized womenswear by South African Thebe Magugu, winner of the 2019 LVMH Prize for Young Fashion Designers; and the joyful intermingling of batik and indigo by Ghanaian Studio One Eighty Nine were all avidly received.

This new wave sweeping the world today is born not only out of an ebullient creativity in Africa, but also out of a powerful force, a singular voice that is rising up and opening a new chapter in fashion, as was the case with the Japanese designers and the Antwerp Six[1] in the 1980s. In her coverage of Imane Ayissi's first Paris Haute Couture show, French journalist Sophie Fontanel writes, "It refreshes the eye and exalts the spirit."[2]

Although Africa has long inspired Western fashion, African designers are now weaving a new aesthetic that reflects a continent-wide demand—for cultural reappropriation and the invention of a language exclusive to Africa. From Cape Town to Abidjan, and from Marrakech to Kigali, designers, photographers, visual artists, and bloggers are shaping what Senegalese sociologist Alioune Sall, in his prescient book *Africa 2025: What Possible Futures for Sub-Saharan Africa?,*[3] calls "a cultural renaissance." In the most optimistic of the four scenarios presented in 2003 by the founder and executive director of the African Futures Institute,[4] Sall writes that this renaissance "allows African societies to look back at their past in a positive light. It allows Africans to mark their territory. It allows them to invent themselves in the world of the twenty-first century." This renaissance champions African cultures, emancipation of the African people, Pan-Africanism, and freedom of expression.

In the mid-1960s, twenty years after World War II, London, riding a wave of economic growth, became the stage for a new lifestyle expressed against a backdrop of demonstrations and sexual liberation. Protesting against the atomic bomb and the Vietnam War—struggles that were evoked in the pop music that flowed from pirate radio stations—the city's youth, middle and working classes alike, shattered establishment codes in their glorification of the right to indulge in pleasure, to exist, and to reinvent the world. Young men started wearing low-rise pants, prints, and psychedelic colors, while women adopted Mary Quant's miniskirt and cropped hairstyles created by Vidal Sassoon. Fashion photographer David Bailey immortalized the model Twiggy; and the clubs on the King's Road thrummed to the beat of the Beatles, the Who, Pink Floyd, and the Rolling Stones. *Time* dedicated its April 15, 1966 issue to the creative ferment sweeping the city. The magazine's cover and an in-depth article cemented the city's reputation with the headline "London: The Swinging City." But Swinging London represented more than just a "lust for life" and baby-boomers' access to consumer goods; it epitomized a cleft in history, a genuine cultural revolution.

It may seem inconceivable to compare a city to a continent, especially considering that Africa is all too often perceived as a single country, and that the West still tends to view Africa through a Eurocentric lens. A shared spirit nevertheless unites the events on London's Carnaby Street in the 1960s with recent developments on the African continent. Fashion designers and photographers, textile designers, makeup artists, and cultural agitators all contribute to shaping this new "Swinging Africa" whose vibrant energy is making waves around the world. Using language to connect these two tectonic historical shifts does not create an artificial relationship, nor amount to a comparison in the strict sense of the term; rather it positions Africa, in London's wake, within the history of fashion, as well as within the history of ideas. For, after all, fashion is not merely sartorial in nature, and the current creative period contributes to what Cameroonian philosopher Achille Mbembe calls "the reversal of the African sign."[5] Fashion may be an industry and a system, but it is first and foremost a means of expression for societies, eras, and people.

In the last fifteen years, African societies have undergone a number of political, economic, demographic, and socio-cultural changes. A middle class has developed in many countries, including Nigeria, Kenya, Ghana, and Ivory Coast. Its members, along with the elite, dictate taste and purchase the products that African cultural entrepreneurs produce. Lifestyles are changing. Without eclipsing traditional tailors, who still hold sway in many circumstances, concept stores and e-commerce sites are multiplying, and they celebrate a new form of fashion design inspired by the continent's diverse cultural heritage. Although many of those with purchasing power continue to favor international brands, this is gradually changing. There was a time, Sall reminds us, "when children who dared to speak the local language in school were forced to wear a dunce cap"—a way of emphasizing that taste has long been shaped by edicts delivered from outside Africa—but now Instagram is flooded with pages urging people to #buyafrican or #wearanafricandesigner.

Fashion weeks in Dakar, Lagos, and Johannesburg[6] have played an important role in the emergence of ready-to-wear. Taking place every year for the past few decades, they have enabled the best designers in Africa to produce together, publicizing their work in Africa and in the world, and securing support from influential individuals. Founded by designers Adama Paris (Senegal), Omoyemi Akerele (Nigeria), and Lucilla Booyzen (South Africa), these events have contributed to generating a new enthusiasm for contemporary African fashion. Some brands have managed to achieve a level of desirability on a par with international labels by being featured in locally produced television series or in Nollywood films,[7] or worn by personalities like Chimamanda Ngozi Adichie (who can often be seen wearing Maki Oh, Nkwo, or Gozel Green), Solange Knowles, and Michelle Obama. In just a few years, the concept store Alara, located in Lagos—a city driving the continent's fashion industry—has become a must-see space and a symbol of the changes at work. Founded by the visionary entrepreneur Reni Folawiyo, this temple to fashion is a pioneer in its field. The store, designed by Anglo-Ghanaian architect David Adjaye, showcases Africa's very best creators alongside some of the world's most cutting-edge designers. Cultural blending's hour has come. In Nigeria's upper circles, fashionable women continue to favor the *aso-ebi*[8] for a friend's wedding, but for a trendy night out will readily pair a *gele*[9] with a Prada dress, or match Louboutin stilettos with a hessian and raffia outfit by Ivorian designer Loza Maléombho.

Yesterday's social strictures are slowly relaxing. In 2020, between 60 and 70 percent of the African population was under thirty. The younger generation, less conditioned by the past and more open to novelty, is accelerating the transformation, much like "repats,"[10] or "third culture kids"[11] who "return home" to the country where their parents or grandparents were from, after growing up in Europe or the United States. The arrival of multi-party systems in the majority of African countries has encouraged a diversity of perspectives. The younger generations feel free to explore new areas of freedom. New technologies no longer open a window onto the West alone; now they introduce these young people to the rest of Africa, and thus to the continent's artists and fashion designers who are stimulating creativity across African borders. Striving to be oneself has become a shared theme. In traditional societies governed by group culture, the "I" is finding a voice without rejecting the "we." While influences have shifted, so have feelings of belonging; donning the symbols of an African culture other than one's own is not an act of cowardice, but rather a celebration—if not a statement. While in a political sense Pan-Africanism remains an ideal, it is the holy grail sought after by all Africans. In a forceful rejection of outside political and economic interference, Africa's youth has found a new role model in Nana Akufo-Addo, the president of Ghana. The author of a highly regarded anticolonial discourse,[12] Addo is also the herald of an Africa liberated from inefficient and alienating systems, a continent that is aware of its own wealth and determined to make something of it.

Ghanaian *batakari* smocks and Kenyan *kikoys*, along with Moroccan djellabas and Senegalese boubous, are all experiencing a revival. Casting aside traditional codes and customs, the younger generation is bringing these garments squarely into fashion while preserving their grandeur. Old postcards, photographs taken in traditional garb, urban and vintage looks, playful cultural reappropriation: Africa's youth uses social media to stage its heritage, blending influences with a certain ingenuity. Under the gaze of photographers and visual artists, the Black body and Black skin—historically subjected to humiliation and mistreatment—become the subjects of new narratives, gradually imposing new aesthetic codes with global influence. Many Instagram accounts celebrate the continent's fashionable figures and their environment, rendering African streets, both in villages and in cities, sexy and fun, and setting the scene in order to assert a proud identity. A powerful wave of creativity is sweeping the continent and beyond, from the Nairobi-based music and fashion festival Thrift Social to music videos by Petite Noir, from the catwalk shows in Lagos to Casablanca's urban music festival L'Boulevard, or from carefully staged images by Laetitia Ky and Tilila Oulhaj to the Afropunk phenomenon.

But does the phrase "African fashion" actually mean anything? Where are the borders of this lexical territory that haphazardly encompasses a boubou made of Senegalese *bazin* cloth, a print dress by Duro Olowu, a wax-print skirt by Parisian brand Maison Château-Rouge, an haute couture dress by Imane Ayissi, the flamboyant wardrobe of dapper Congolese *sapeurs*, bold designs by Nigerian label Orange Culture, an intricate Moroccan caftan, and the late Nelson Mandela's shirts, created for him by the Burkinabe designer Pathé O? What do the words "African fashion" mean when some in the West still—at the dawn of the third decade of the twenty-first century—struggle to acknowledge the "Africanness" of garments such as a navy-blue linen dress from Lagos-based womenswear brand Meena, because, according to them, there is nothing African—or "ethnic"—about the fabric, color, or form, even though the subtle origami effects that enliven the silhouette are symbolically rooted in the designer's Igbo culture? This inscrutability, which the artisans and designers themselves sometimes cultivate through skillfully orchestrated phenomena of resistance, startles the Western gaze and way of thinking, which are all too accustomed to the stereotyped images that have structured them. Dress codes differ from Dakar to Nairobi to Cairo. Carina style,[13] a "modest" and colorful fashion popular in Egypt, bears no resemblance to the low waists and *ndokette* dresses that are essential pieces in the traditional Senegalese woman's wardrobe. Garments like the iconic dashiki[14] tunic, created by Vlisco in 1963—and dusted off from time to time by certain women's fashion magazines to illustrate a supposedly "African" style—are more the prerogative of large community gatherings within African diasporas scattered around the world (who made the tunic famous), rather than a "style" commonly worn in Africa.

There is no African fashion; there are African designers, with their visions, concepts, and fantasies. In Lagos, Nigerian designer Bubu Ogisi, founder of fashion brand I.AM. ISIGO, summons Congolese deities and Ashanti queens, drawing inspiration for her stories and techniques from the cultural heritage of a continent that she is constantly exploring. In doing so, she weaves an "art-house fashion" in which the craftsperson plays a central role in rebuilding the world. With an innate sense of style, Dakar-based Sarah Diouf strives to create a mainstream African brand with fashion-forward designs that feature bold graphics and are entirely crafted in a local workshop. In Cape Town, Laduma Ngxokolo's label Maxhosa revisits traditional patterns from Xhosa culture, giving them new life in knitwear made with South African wool and mohair. Ngxokolo's casual, sophisticated fashion is imbued with the values that were passed on to the designer during the traditional Xhosa initiation for men, the experience that inspired the label. In addition to his bespoke pieces, Oswald Boateng—a master tailor on London's Savile Row and the son of Ghanaian parents—designs a ready-to-wear collection called "Africanism." The tone-on-tone use of small motifs found on kente cloth and traditional textiles, usually worn by Ashanti nobles and the Ewe people, sets richly colored cottons and silks shimmering. None of these brands is alike. Yet each, in its unique way—whether in the fold of a garment, the weft of a woven cloth, or the vibrancy of a color—articulates a shared ideal: the deconstruction of myths and the invention of an Africanness defined by the continent and its diasporas themselves.

The vast majority of African designers living and working on the continent face many challenges, as their environment, with few exceptions, provides too little support for the fashion industry. Weak textile infrastructure, a lack of training opportunities, an underqualified local workforce, and a scarcity of public and private investment weigh heavily on the sector. And then there is Africa's white gold—the best cotton in the world; produced in Mali or Burkina Faso, it is heavily exported and rarely processed locally. The manufacturing process is extremely expensive for local designers, who are forced to import thread, tools, and other raw materials. On top of that, the cost of exporting finished products is so high, even to other African countries, that it undermines sales. The sector's strength lies in the handicraft of the artisans endowed with precious, time-honored techniques. Africa holds treasures—something the Western world knows all too well. And if luxury is defined by slow fashion, handmade goods, culture, art, and history, then African textile crafts—*métiers d'art* every bit as worthy as those that have forged the reputations of the world's most prestigious fashion houses—are the quintessence of luxury.

The first chapter of this book reveals the fierce desire that drives fashion designers to preserve their artisanal heritage. They personally reflect on ways to revitalize the industry and convince consumers to adopt new practices. Socially conscious, many of them have adopted a sustainable approach to fashion by practicing upcycling, which is rooted in traditional culture, before it became a trend. Their collections are charged with meaning and narratives that breathe new life into fashion at a time when the world's markets are saturated with soulless products. Each collection is a modern tale that summons up the past as much as it speaks to the present, giving form to a richly textured promise and offering something to reflect upon as well as something to wear. This approach reminds us that the mere fact that we can't see something doesn't mean it doesn't exist, and the fact that we don't understand something doesn't make it meaningless. This generation has something new to offer; it is wiping the slate clean and ensuring that we sit up and pay attention, that we listen carefully. Fashion everywhere has always had the power to transform us. The new face of African fashion has the power to reinvent the way we look at the world.

But let's not idealize things: in the same way that not everyone benefited from the jubilation of Swinging London, for the moment the sweet taste of cultural revolution only concerns a minority of Africans—although they are an active and influential minority. To paraphrase Alioune Sall's hope, expressed in *Africa 2025*,[15] this generation is realizing that faithfulness to oneself lies in movement. Lafalaise Dion, Ivorian designer of headdresses and jewelry; South African visual artist Trevor Stuurman; Oliver Asike, creator of the socially active Kenyan label Vitimbi and founder of a festival that combines music and fashion; Joseph Ouechen, creator of "No Couscous," anti-stereotype photographs about Morocco; Senegalese designer Selly Raby Kane; Nigerian photographer Stephen Tayo: each of these artists, in their own way, is revitalizing international fashion and African spheres through a decolonialized yet diverse practice. They "approximate the fashion performance to almost a phenomenology of African presence," according to Italian researcher Enrica Picarelli.[16] Independent and uncompromising, freed from the need to exist within a framework, these designers are telling stories rather than selling products. Their creative work sews up the torn pieces of the past, while at the same time imposing a vocabulary and tackling the age-old imbalances that have, until now, excluded it from the "validated" and "validating" circles of fashion.

"I need no validation," declares Adama Paris, designer and founder of Dakar Fashion Week and the Black Fashion Experience in Paris. The freedom and boldness, courage and convictions of Africa's new generation of creatives have given Africans a reflection of their own worth, which they were sorely missing,[17] and are unblocking Western thinking about African fashion, and about the continent as a whole. It is not only clothing or images that they are creating, but also the future.

Louis Philippe de Gagoue—the prince of African fashion, as well as its enfant terrible—was one of the first contributors to send his images, yet he will never see this completed book. As the finishing touches were being carried out, he passed away before his time, leaving a community of friends, artists, and admirers inconsolable.

With his distinctive style, his dazzling imagination, and his talent for photography—his signature was unmistakable—he was and always will be one of the most inspiring African photographers of the early twenty-first century.

"May the ground be light to you,"* little brother from Yaoundé and Abidjan.

* A farewell and expression of respect uttered at funerals in French-speaking West Africa.

T

Traditional African textiles—a term that typically evokes fabrics that are handwoven, hand-painted, or hand-dyed—have been perceived, depending on who is speaking, and where, either as an added value, a constraint, or a confine. But consider the work of Tunisian designer Azzedine Alaïa or Malian label XULY.Bët, and it becomes immediately apparent that the creations of African designers cannot, and must not, be reduced to the use of textiles that are ostensibly traditional.

In fact, since the 1970s, many African designers—especially in West Africa—have sought to develop their heritage and foster interactions between contemporary fashion and the raw materials and textile traditions of Africa. When Malian designer Chris Seydou, who pioneered a movement that has never lost momentum, cut an above-the-knee pencil skirt out of *bogolan* fabric, it was a revolution—a cultural revolution. No one had ever dared to work with this fabric, imbued with social and protective powers, reserved for special occasions, and considered highly symbolic by the Bambara people. *Bogolan*—a woven cotton fabric dyed with mud in earthy colors, a loquacious living material covered with an ancient, codified graphic vocabulary—is a national symbol. Chris Seydou glorified the printed symbols' telluric power in small structured jackets with Eighties-style shoulders and defined waists, and in bell-bottomed pants. Masterfully mixing and matching motifs, he combined or overlapped polka dots, circles, diamonds, and squares—mysterious symbols illegible to the uninitiated eye. Seydou elevated *bogolan* to "couture." During this period, many couturiers emerged (thanks to Seydou, they were no longer referred to as "tailors," but as "couturiers"), who would in turn work with *ndop* cloth, Faso Dan Fani, cotton *bazin* fabrics, *ntchak* cloth, flatweave *kilims,* and cloth from the Kasai River region.

TEXTILES, TECHNIQUES, AND INNOVATION

Left:
Emmy Kasbit (brand created by Emmanuel Okoro), pants and tunic from the fall–winter 2020 collection.
© Michael Oshai.

Facing page:
Tiffany Amber (brand created by Folake Coker), skirt, top, and dress from the spring–summer 2018 collection, modeled by Tolulope Ethmalosa Balogun and Ifeoma Nwobu.
Courtesy Tiffany Amber.

Designers Ly Dumas (Cameroon), Alphadi (Nigeria), Kofi Ansah (Ghana), and Oumou Sy (Senegal), among others, combine the sacred and the practical, and draw on the flamboyance of African kingdoms, the prestige of traditional chiefdoms, the know-how of castes, and the mystery of secret societies and the popular arts to create a subversive kind of poetry. Forty years later, the number of designers present at the most respected fashion weeks—both on the African continent and in Paris and New York—who draw on their cultural, textile, and artisanal heritage to spin their own creative fibers continues to grow. The world has changed. Plastic is now woven into cotton *bazin* fabrics[1]; stretch fabric gives body to Senegalese woven pagnes; *adire*—a cotton cloth dyed with a "resist" technique unique to the Yoruba people of Nigeria—engulfs silk dresses and diaphanous blouses; and Xhosa beadwork inspires knitted creations. *Akwete*, *adire*, kente, cracking, *akwa-ocha*, *sfifa*, *netela*, indigo, batik, felt, raffia, *tapa*, nacre, and trim are all infused with modernity thanks to the creative designs of Imane Ayissi, Emmy Kasbit, Studio One Eighty Nine, Maxhosa, Nourredine Amir, Lem-Lem, Mafi Mafi, Sadafa, Post Imperial, Tsemaye Binitie, Maki Oh, and Tiffany Amber.

The dreams and the aesthetic approach of these pioneering designers have been coupled with another aim: to innovate in order to secure a firm footing in the future. "We will continue to lose the custodians of our traditional craft skills if we do not find a permanent and sustainable way to preserve them; and the best way to do that is through innovation," notes Nigerian designer Nkwo Onwuka, founder of the label NKWO. Like other forward-looking initiatives, the label strives to promote *aso-oke* and Nigerian woven cottons,

Left:
Designs by Seidnaly Sidhamed, known as Alphadi, published in *Revue Noire* (no. 27, December 1997).
© Courtesy Revue Noire/ N'Goné Fall.

Above:
Oumou Sy, dress, headscarf, and accessories, Dakar Fashion Week, Senegal, 2012.
© REUTERS/Finbarr O'Reilly.

Facing page:
Chris Seydou, *bogolan* ensemble (1996), modeled by Bintou Konaté, 2021.
Emmanuelle Courrèges private collection.
© Olivier Marty.

in this case by creating a signature fabric, *dakala*, which is made of strips of recycled denim and woven cotton and resembles handwoven cloth (see p. 47). (see p. 47) The way to preserve craft skills and offer new possibilities to the African fashion industry is to create brands with strong added value. There was a time when *aso-oke*—a traditional Yoruba woven cloth said to date from the tenth century—was a blend of cotton and silk; the silkworm cocoons were incubated and sorted locally, and the threads combed and spun in the west and southwest regions of the country. Today, these materials are often replaced by rayon, which has certainly made weaving more accessible, including outside of the Yoruba community, but it has also jeopardized the craft. The development of "fast craft," the arrival of imported Chinese copies, and the fact that certain communities of craftspeople have abandoned these major art forms, which no longer provide sufficient income, have mobilized fashion designers. Kenneth Ize began presenting at Paris fashion weeks in January 2020 and introduced *aso-oke* to luxury ready-to-wear. For his spring–summer 2021 collection, he had pineapple motifs embroidered on bayadere cloth, an innovative and multi-layered display of craftsmanship created between the city of Ilorin in northern Nigeria, where he established a workshop of thirty weavers, and the valleys of Tyrol, in Austria (he grew up in Austria). In 2019, he paired his woven fabrics with silk printed with artwork by Nigerian artist Fadekemi Ogunsanya: women's faces framed by medallions, forming a pattern in shades of blue that is reminiscent—through the designer's use of mise en abyme—of certain West African textiles, namely the repeated motifs in batik fabrics and the use of indigo. Emmy Kasbit followed the same approach: over a span of several collections, the label appropriated another Nigerian cloth, *akwete*—symbolic of the Igbo culture and exhibiting more than one hundred identified patterns—to create a joyful wardrobe infused with a rock-n-roll spirit.

Fully aware of the issues associated with textiles in Africa, these designers know that preserving craft skills will take more than simply adapting them to "the spirit of the times." "The only way to revive [those things] is . . . also to be forward-thinking,"[2] asserts Kenneth

Abiola Olusola, embroidered blouse from the spring–summer 2019 collection, modeled by Mabel Okpara.
© Michael Oshai.

Ize. Take Lisa Folawiyo: fascinated by *ankara* (the name for wax-print fabric in Nigeria), the designer used this imported fabric, connected with the expansion of European trade, as the foundation for a creative, sustainable project celebrating handicraft, embroidery, and dyes. In this deconstructive exercise in which traditional techniques like *adire* are skillfully overlaid on wax-print fabric, each glittering bead and sequin outlining the motifs underscores the promise of these metamorphoses. And so a precious, distinctive cloth is born—one that casts a spell from Lagos to New York. In Bamako, Awa Meité also set out to create her own textile identity. Through skillful collaboration with craftspeople who possess a wealth of knowledge passed down to them by previous masters, she created woven patterns that are easily identifiable today. Some of these patterns emerged from what the weavers initially considered "errors"; the designer showed them how to reconsider their perspective by casting off the "rules." Awa Meité conceived other patterns, such as *tigani*—"peanut" in the Bambara language—as she watched the craftspeople snack on peanuts while they worked. Her signature lies in the way she uses innovative material and textural effects to give voice to her cottons. In 2016, Senegalese designer Sophie Nzinga Sy also contributed to this forward momentum when she turned the country's emblematic woven pagne cloth into a devilishly sexy, pliable material. She uses it to design narrow skirts and sheath dresses that appear to be molded onto women's bodies, thanks to the help of textile designer Johanna Bramble, who heads a Dakar-based Manjak weaving workshop that blends pagne cloth with stretch fabric. The Nigerian label Lagos Space Programme has undertaken a similar project by collaborating with a textile studio to knit blouses and sweaters from strips of cotton derived from fabric dyed with indigo using the *adire* technique. The equally daring Cameroonian designer Imane Ayissi and Nigerian Bubu Ogisi, of the label I.AM.ISIGO, have undertaken the task of restoring *obom* to its former glory; this textile made by shredding and beating tree bark is still highly associated with rural zones in Cameroon, the Ivory Coast, and Uganda, and for this reason often remains unknown in fashion circles.

Details of dresses from Noureddine Amir's fall–winter 2018 collection, presented at the Institut du Monde Arabe, Paris Fashion Week, July 2, 2018.
© Imaxtree.

Below:
Lisa Folawiyo,
details of embroidery
work, 2016.
© Emmanuelle Courrèges.

Right
and facing page:
Lisa Folawiyo, looks
from the "COLL 1
2020" collection.
© Olabisi Olaleye.
Courtesy Lisa Folawiyo.

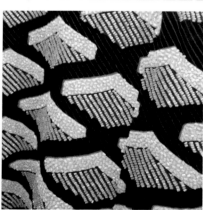

There could have been no better comeback for *obom* than its appearance at Paris Haute Couture Fashion Week in January 2020: flower petals made of bark, hand-painted and edged with Swarovski crystal, formed collars and plastrons of astounding beauty on dresses of white, yellow, gray, and black silk designed by Imane Ayissi. This tree bark appeared more casual-chic in the I.AM.ISIGO collection, where it was worked like leather, its warm, smoky tones enhanced by Bubu Ogisi's innate sense of style.

"The job of a designer is to transform," says Karim Adduchi. In the nimble fingers of this young Moroccan designer, who was invited to show his ready-to-wear collection at Paris Fashion Week in spring 2019, Moroccan *handira*—the celebrated Berber wedding blanket—becomes a sheath dress; *zellij* mosaics metamorphose into an embroidered bodice; traditional carpets, either in knotted wool or industrial versions in plastic or nylon, are turned into oversize deconstructed skirts. Sometimes it takes a daring break with tradition to convince people of the importance of preserving heritage: in her spring–summer 2016 collection, Ivorian designer Loza Maléombho used raffia details inspired by Zauli masks from the eastern part of the country to emphasize the wrists, busts, and hips of her designs. Imane Ayissi uses the same raffia to dress elegant women in knitted couture sheath dresses or little capes to enhance lamé dresses. Amine Bendriouich also began breaking boundaries early on. In a collection called "Ich Bin Ein Berberliner," an ode to the cultural blending he has always cultivated in his work, he infuses frock coats, wrap skirts, and trailing black gowns with embroidery typical of M'hamid Ighizlane, which traditionally ornaments the headscarves of young married women from this region of the Moroccan Sahara. Whether strewing his sweatshirts with *aaka* buttons (treasures of Moroccan passementerie) or embroidering seventy-five jackets sold as a limited edition at Paris concept store Colette[3] with patterns inspired by the costumes worn by Gnawa musicians, the mischievous but socially committed Amine Bendriouich intends "to free traditional craftsmanship from stereotypes."[4] A certain distance is necessary to lift craft skills out of tradition and folklore, so that craftspeople and clients—both local and international—might imagine them differently, and appreciate and adopt them in other circles and on new occasions. "It's important that my work preserve heritage, but it must also create a new economic model based on a balance between craft and industry," he says.

Twenty years ago, in her work *Mille Tisserands en Quête d'Avenir* (A Thousand Weavers Seeking a Future),[5] Mali's former minister of culture Aminata Dramane Traoré questioned the impact of this shared ideal. "Can we expect African fashion to pull the African textile sector up with it? Is the fashion phenomenon sufficiently anchored in custom to be able to play this leavening role?" The enthusiasm of the subsequent generations and their renewed pride is proof enough that Africa has already met this challenge. Designers are not only creating clothes; they are crafting a new world, woven with messages and ideas. Where the economy is meaningful, a future exists.

Left:
Kenneth Ize, shirt and pants from the "A Man's Only as Good as His Words" collection, spring–summer 2021, Paris Fashion Week, October 1, 2020.
© Kristy Sparow/Getty Images.

Facing page:
Kenneth Ize, suits and scarves from the fall–winter 2019 collection.
© Stephen Tayo.

Above:
Fadekemi Ogunsanya,
Untitled, 2019,
gouache on paper,
16½ × 23⅓ in.
(42 × 59.4 cm).

Facing page:
Kenneth Ize, long silk
shirt featuring a work
created by Nigerian
artist Fadekemi
Ogunsanya, Arise
Fashion Week, Lagos,
Nigeria, April 2019.

"I use the art of making garments or textiles as a form of ritual or meditation. The amount of time and effort that goes into creating something by hand generates a deeper feeling than something created using a machine. In this way, we preserve not only our legacy, but also the stories that we tell by making them authentic. It is a unique way to decolonize the mind and create a free space to understand what has been, what is, and what is to come. For the collection 'Chasing Evil,' I was inspired by *nkisi nkondi* statuettes: totems believed to protect against evil that I discovered in Congo. Nigeria, my home country, and Congo are very similar in terms of how much they value dress, which can be used as a sign of protection. The Congolese dandies use the art of dressing up to create a shield of rebellion or protection, as well as to make a fashion statement. This collection reflects the cohesive synergy of different details that contribute to chasing evil."

Bubu Ogisi
DESIGNER AND FOUNDER OF THE BRAND I.AM.ISIGO
@iamisigo

I.AM.ISIGO, pant suit from the "Chasing Evil" collection, fall–winter 2020, modeled by Gabriella Duduh. Styling: Sunny Dolat. Makeup: Jamie Kimani.
© Maganga Mwagogo.

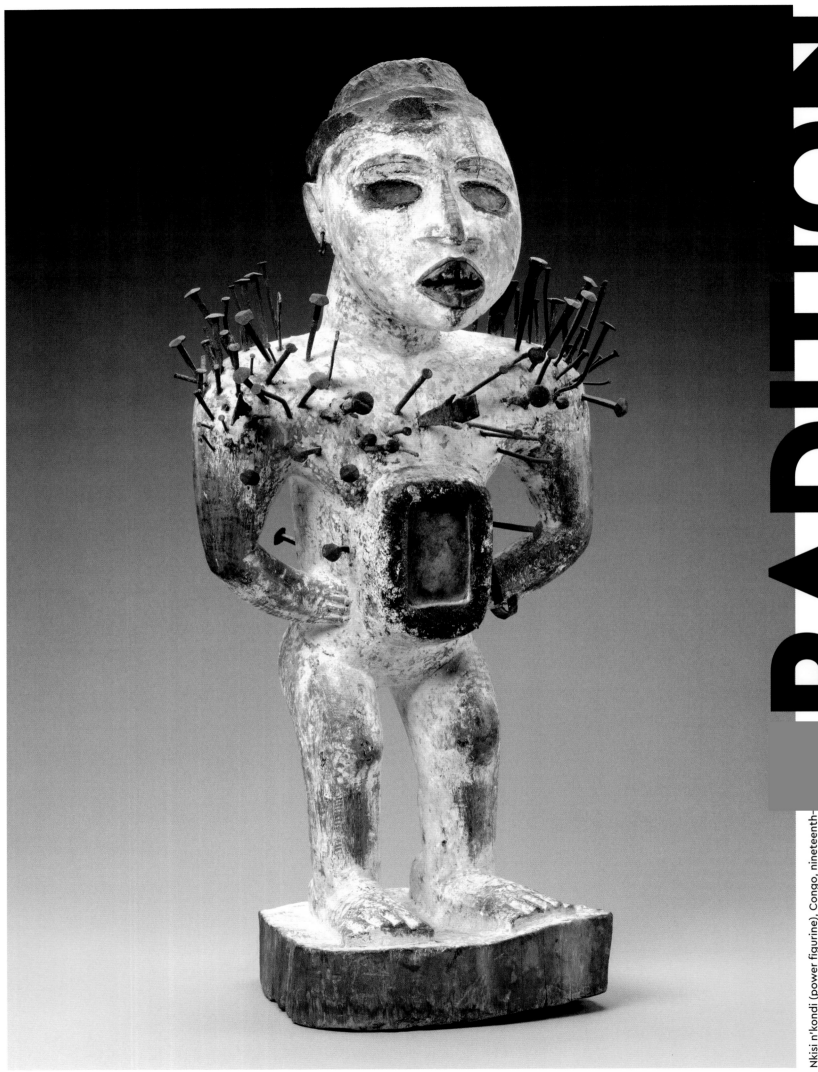

Nkisi n'kondi (power figurine), Congo, nineteenth–
twentieth century, wood, glass, iron nails, pigment
and sacred materials, 24 × 12 in. (61 × 30.5 cm).

from the "Chasing Evil" collection, fall-winter 2020, modeled by Gabriella Duduh. Styling: Sunny Dolat. Makeup: Jamie Kimani. © Maganga Mwagogo.

TREND

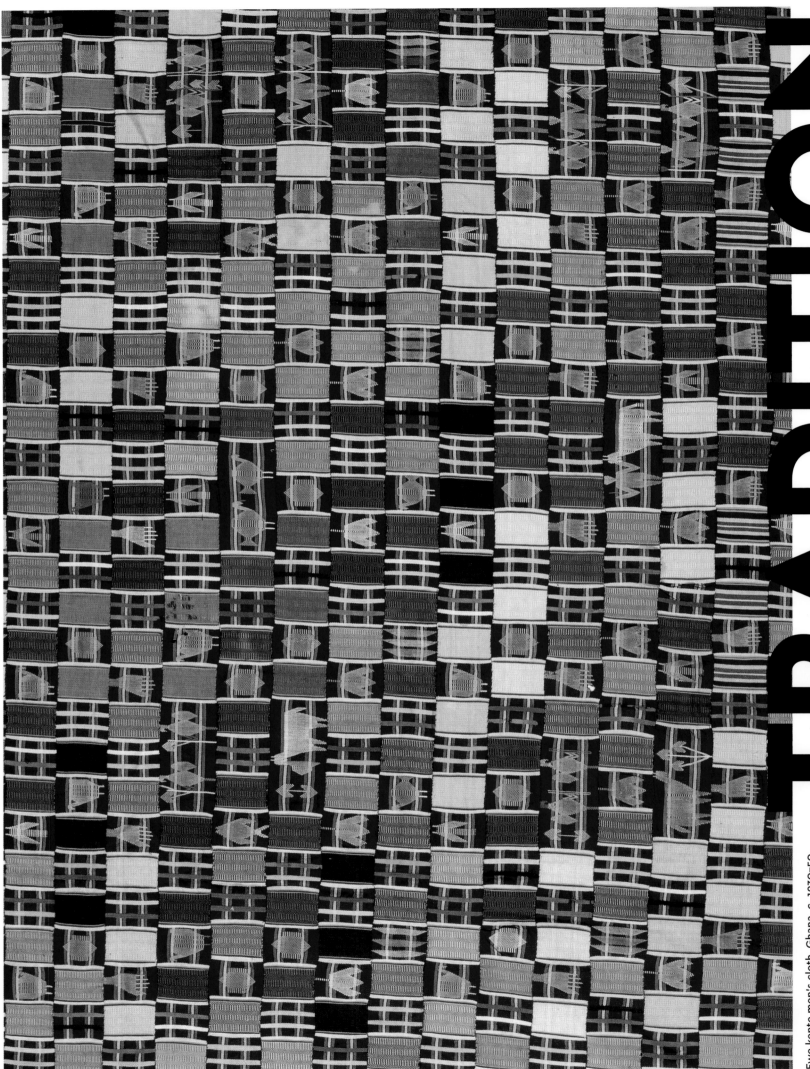

Ewe kente men's cloth, Ghana, c. 1930–50.
© Adire African Textiles, London.

TREND

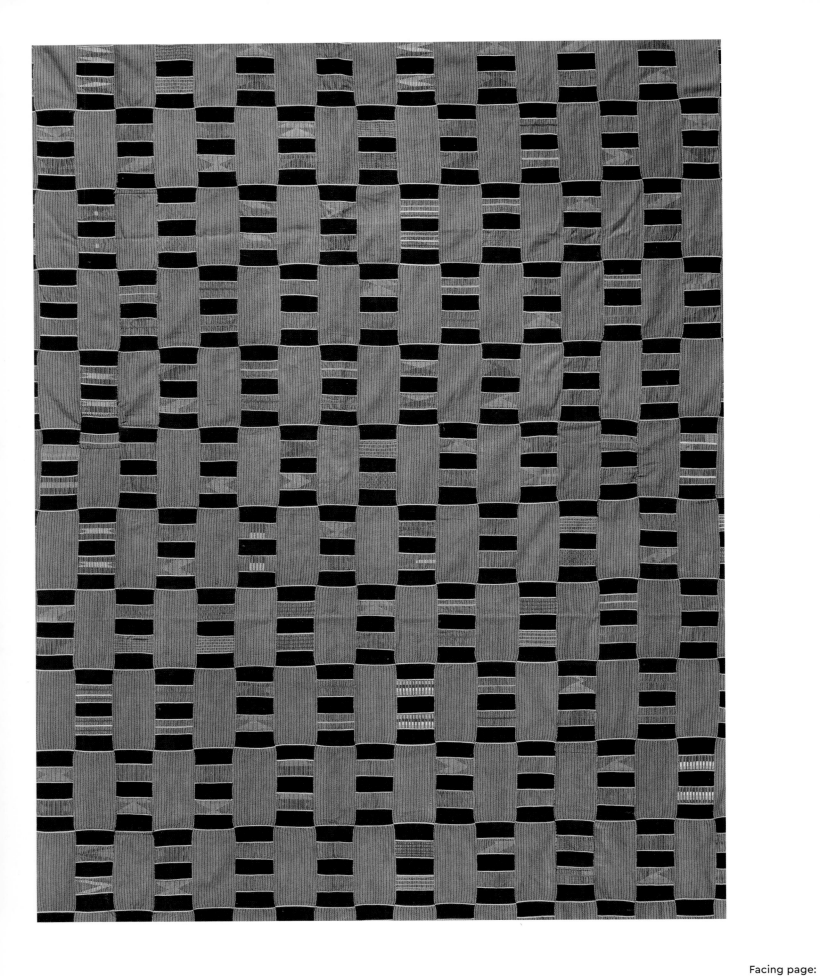

Above:
Ewe kente men's
cloth, original
variation in soft green
of a popular style
of kente in Ghana.

Facing page:
Adire fabric, dyed
with a technique
used by the Yoruba
people, featuring a
hand-drawn *olokun*
design, whose name
is derived from the
goddess of wealth,
Nigeria, c. 1960.

Page 46:
Lagos Space Programme (brand created by Adeju Thompson), knitted cape-blouse and pants from the "Project 5" capsule collection, modeled by Toby Akinyosoye, 2021.
© Kadara Enyeasi.

Page 47:
NKWO (brand created by Nkwo Onwuka), dress in *dakala* fabric and sandals from the spring–summer 2018 collection.
© Chinasa Opara Photography.

Facing page:
Sophie Nzinga Sy, sheath dress from the spring–summer 2016 collection, in pagne fabric woven by Johanna Bramble.
© Delphine Diallo.

Above:
Awa Meité, cotton ensemble, modeled by Fadima Konate.
Hair and makeup:
Awa Meité Design.
© Coralie Coco.

Below:
Imane Ayissi, bustier dress in silk and *tapa* cloth from the spring–summer 2020 haute couture collection, Paris Fashion Week.
© François Lenoir/Reuters.

Facing page:
I.AM.ISIGO (brand created by Bubu Ogisi), dress in *tapa* cloth from the "Supreme Higher Entity" collection, spring–summer 2020, modeled by Tatiana Sinon. Art direction, hair, and makeup: Bubu Ogisi.
© Kader Diaby.

Zaouli mask from Tibéita, in the Marahoué region of Ivory Coast, 2015. © Aka Konin. © Office Ivoirien du Patrimoine Culturel (OIPC), 2015.

TREND

Loza Maléombho, dress in hessian and raffia from the "Zaouli" collection, spring-summer 2016. © Daniel Sery

TRADITION

Kalin mask from the village of Balavé, at the 20th
International Festival of Masks and the Arts (FESTIMA)
in Dedougou, Burkina Faso, 2014. © Jacob Balzani Lööv.

Imane Ayissi, look from the "Akouma" collection, spring–summer 2020, modeled by Luca Adamik (City Models agency).

TREND

Above:
Amine Bendriouich,
cotton hoodie
embroidered with
aakad buttons,
from the "Mr. Joy"
series, 2019.
© Yoriyas Yassine Alaoui.

Facing page:
Amine Bendriouich,
"Gnawa Bomb Blue"
bomber jacket from
the "Gnawa Bombs"
collection, 2016.
© Hassan Hajjaj.
Courtesy of the artist.

Since the late 1990s, the word "ethnic" has been used by the fashion media to refer to a set of styles and garments displaying the objective and subjective characteristics of a country or continent. African designers are subjected to paradoxical dictates: to gain recognition, they seem obligated to provide proof of their Africanness—"to appear African"—while being excluded from the fashion arena when this proof is perceived by the West as being "too ethnic." The Nest Collective, a Kenyan multidisciplinary arts collective, published *Not African Enough*,[1] a book whose title speaks to the violence of having the very contours of one's identity imposed upon. When asked about the interactions that he so enjoys developing between textiles from Africa and the rest of the world—kente cloth from Ghana and silk from Japan, Faso Dan Fani from Burkina Faso and calendered indigo created by the Miao women of China—Cameroonian designer Imane Ayissi likes to remind people that "putting the Eiffel Tower in all your prints doesn't make for French fashion."[2] The Africa of African designers is not a physical destination or a fantasy, but an emotional attachment to a heritage. Breaking free from conventions, each invents their own world and deploys a language of the initiated, in a joyful attempt to escape labels.

As African countries gained their independence during the process of decolonization, not everyone on the continent seemed to adhere to the spirit of "Abacost" (the abbreviation for *à bas le costume*, literally "down with the suit"), a sartorial movement initiated by President Mobutu in 1971 as part of his policy of "Zairianization," or authenticity.[3] However, it was at work in many places and in various different forms, and could be seen in the creations of numerous designers. Inventing your own vocabulary—being yourself—is not always about breaking with the constraints imposed upon you, but rather about making something of them. The history of African textiles demonstrates that, in many cases, well ahead of fashion designers—and statesmen like Keïta, Mobutu, NKrumah, Sankara, or Mandela[4]—craftspeople themselves

INVENTING A LANGUAGE

undertook the deconstruction of imported products, in defiance or resistance, and to preserve a certain "aesthetic independence and cultural sovereignty."[5] In the 1830s, for example, the Kalabari women of Nigeria, who had adopted Indian madras cotton (which they called *injiri*), modified the patterns in the fabric by removing selected threads. Through this "subtraction" process, they produced new "signature" textiles with highly codified designs called *pelete bite*.[6] In 2019, designer Ituen Basi set about reinventing this same madras cotton, known as "George" to the Igbo people of northern Nigeria,[7] using various textile "blending" processes in "Dear George," a feminine collection with a touch of humor. Her patchwork approach, which combines several madras patterns, and her way of softening the geometric lines with openwork lace or of introducing cultural elements (cowry shells, grigri belts) contribute—like the Kalabari women's work—to creating entirely new, unique pieces that reflect history and criticism, while also taking a step back. Although they rarely use this terminology (which is more the preserve of researchers and teachers), many African designers create "decolonial" fashion, in which numerous methods of resistance intertwine.

This same notion of shared spirit and identity is present in Lisa Folawiyo's spring–summer 2018 collection, "Kwenu."[8] The designer drew inspiration from the

Lisa Folawiyo, look from the spring–summer 2018 collection, modeled by Rebecca Fabunmi.
© Willy Verse (William Ukoh).

patterns on the traditional Okpu agu hats[9] worn by Igbo men to infuse her jewel-tone silk dresses and blouses with a spirit of bravery. Through this shift, she celebrates the courage and power of women, investing them with even more by combining these patterns with lion's head prints borrowed from the same repertory. By dressing women in the feline motifs that decorate male Isi-agu tunics[10] traditionally worn by men who have been given the title of chief, Lisa Folawiyo shakes things up, unraveling cosmogonies and stitching them back together. From these gleaming golden manes, she invents a feminist and subversive form of fashion that draws its power from myth, a far cry from what Western fashion might perceive as a "jungle" motif.

Even if this remains imperceptible to the untrained eye, Western forms are all subject to reinterpretation. This is what Imane Ayissi sought to relate and celebrate in his spring–summer 2018 haute couture collection, "Heroes": a tribute to the resilience of the Herero women of Namibia, who were victims of the first genocide of the twentieth century, committed by the German colonial army. "Even today, the women's outfits are a legacy of that tragic period, with empire waists, gigot sleeves, gathered skirts, and incredible volumes. And yet, there is something very personal, very unique about this display that is specific to them. It is both a record of a period and, at the same time, I see in it a domination over history, an incredible resistance. They've been able to reinvent their clothing and invest it with their own colors, in every sense of the word, transcending and sublimating this painful heritage through fashion," explains the designer.[11] Regardless of its motivation, fashion everywhere will always be nothing more than co-creation or re-creation. The colorful patchwork fabrics characteristic of the contemporary Herero woman's wardrobe symbolize the multitude of influences running through our lives: in the designer's reinterpretation, up to 234 pieces of fabric may be assembled to create a skirt.

Fashion is hybrid by nature; many designers, such as Senegalese Selly Raby Kane, play on this to create new aesthetics. Heavily influenced by science fiction, fantasy, and cartoons, as much as by

Below:
Ituen Basi, look from the "Dear George" collection, Arise Fashion Week, Lagos, Nigeria, April 21, 2019.
© Bennett Raglin/Getty Images.

Facing page:
Selly Raby Kane, look from the "Dakar City of Birds" collection, fall–winter 2015.
© Jean-Baptiste Joire.

Facing page:
Amine Bendriouich,
look from the
"Djellabas & Tricks"
collection, 2020.
Courtesy Amine Bendriouich.

Above:
BLOKE (brand created
by Faith Oluwajimi),
looks from the "Family
Portrait" collection,
spring–summer 2020.
© Kola Oshalusi/Insigna Media.

subcultures in Dakar, the designer draws from seemingly contradictory lexicons (cultural, visual, and textile) to create her own artistic language. In combining a kimono and *bazin* cotton; in reinventing the art of embroidery—highly symbolic and rooted in Senegalese sartorial culture—using imaginative appliqués that borrow swallow or fan motifs from Vlisco's well-known wax-print fabrics[12]; in trimming a plastic skirt with a braid of hair; or in using a sweater or a dress to celebrate the recycling culture of the Baye Fall, a sub-group of Senegal's Sufi Muslim community, the Mourides,[13] Selly Raby Kane creates a Creole language as defined by Édouard Glissant: "A blending of arts or languages that produces something unexpected, . . . a way of continually transforming oneself without losing oneself. . . . A space where dispersion enables togetherness, where culture shock, imbalance, disorder, and interference become creative elements."[14] With her surrealistic fantasies that straddle loyalty and autonomy, conservatism and futurism, integration and oneirism, Selly Raby Kane challenges the eyes and the very definition of African fashion.

Above:
Emmy Kasbit (brand created by Emmanuel Okoro), look from the "Memories: Part II" collection, fall–winter 2019, modeled by Oreva Buwa.
© Onyinye Fafi Obi.

Right:
Meena (brand created by Uju Offiah), look from the "Ochiagha" collection, spring–summer 2016, Lagos Fashion Week, Nigeria, 2015.
© Kola Oshalusi/Insigna Media.

Facing page:
Maxivive (brand founded by Papa Oyeyemi), jacket, tunic, hat, bag, and sandals from the "Pre-Wet" collection, 2020, modeled by Dior Bonou.
© Kosol Onwudinjor.
Courtesy Maxivive.

Similarly, Imane Ayissi uses figures "in the style of" those adorning Ghanaian Asafo flags to convey modern messages ("Save the Oceans," "Save the Planet," "Save the Forest") on silk douppioni evening dresses. Sewn using the appliqué technique, these small figures, including whales, trees, and flowers, belong to this ancient heritage—a textile treasure inherited from the Fanti[15] military companies that used them in their struggle against colonial oppression. Whether using a naïve style to symbolize proverbs or recounting historical events, today they convey more peaceful messages to the community—a means for the designer to raise a truly African voice committed to defending the environment.

Created by the young Franco-Sudanese designer Abdel El Tayeb, the equally African collection "Ma Nation Porte Ton Nom" [My Nation Bears Your Name] is a tribute to the designer's father, who suffered an untimely death. El Tayeb explores questions of cultural hybridity and identity, and the difficulty Africans have with projecting themselves into white society. Raised in Bordeaux, in France, he has invented a nation "with its own standard, flag, uniform, and medals" (see p. 9). From nostalgic memories of his native Sudan and women wearing the traditional *thobe* tunic at weddings—looking, in his words, "magnificent, radiant, joyful"—he created a majestic procession inspired both by French military uniforms and by the color and texture of date palm basketry, a craft his two grandmothers taught him. The designer wanted to explore "the idea of fertility, transmission, of what we give to our children." His curvy, maternal-looking designs feature elements of basket weaving and are inspired by Giacometti's famous *Spoon Woman*, whose form is powerfully evocative of African statues, and maternity. Abdel El Tayeb gives new proportions to the female body that contain the seed of an idea: garments with meaning.

Fashion is a forest resonating with voices and words. Nigerian brands Maki Oh, BLOKE, Tiffany Amber, Gozel Green, Meena, Emmy Kasbit, and Maxivive regularly make use of alphabets in their creations. Dyed, printed, or woven, bestowed with narrative or playful qualities, the designers' letters redefine the traditional use of symbols on textiles: a family tree diagram and anagrams of the word "family" in BLOKE's spring–summer 2020 collection; proverbs and the names of the four market days (Eke, Orie, Afro, Nkwo) that punctuate the *izu*—the Igbo word for "week"—in Emmy Kasbit's designs; interactive wordplay by Gozel Green; or Nsibidi[16] by Meena. "With *adire*, it's always used as a hidden conversation about the collection,"[17] says Amaka Osakwe of the label Maki Oh. Other brands, like Gozel Green, offer a liberated space and break the rules governing the concept of fabric-as-messenger, while injecting them with a dose of humor, distance, and play. "The choice of letters of the alphabet and words we employed in this collection allows viewers to explore them as puzzles, and to

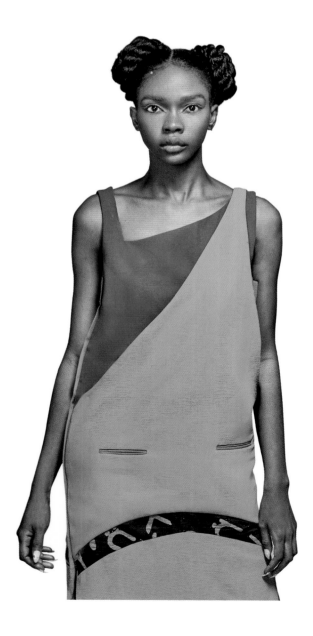

68.

Gozel Green
(brand created by
Sylvia Enekwe-Ojei
and Olivia Enekwe-
Okoji), looks from the
"Writings on the Wall"
collection,
fall–winter 2020.
© Favour Benjamin.

arrive at varying meanings," says Olivia Enekwe-Ojei, one of the founders of the label, in reference to the fall–winter 2020 collection, "Writings on the Wall." At Gozel Green, color is also a language, visual and eloquent, with a palette rooted less in the symbolism of individual hues than in the culture of color among the Igbo people. For many African designers, deconstruction is a project, culture is a vocabulary, subversion is emancipation, and illegibility can at times be resistance.

Illegible and invisible: these are precisely the notions that Karim Adduchi wanted to capture and explore in his collection "She Knows Why the Caged Bird Sings," as well as to translate the mystical spirit that escapes the eye and the power behind the material. In an homage to the craftswomen in his native Imzouren region of Morocco, the designer drew inspiration from their lifestyle and emblematic pieces that have stood the test of time in a dizzying array of textures and colors, enriched by stories and knowledge. "Those women

seen from the outside world often seem weak, but their strength is hidden in their humbleness. They have no need to expose their powers to prove themselves. And that was something that shocked me, because, in the Western culture, exposing your powers is obvious. However, in Arab and Moroccan culture, creating equality and togetherness is how you gain strength," he comments.

The "Africanness" of these creations lies not in archetypes, but in their singular lexicon and the ideas that infuse them. This is also what gives them their innovative if not revolutionary quality. Some still claim there is no written transmission in Africa and that the oral tradition is the only way to tell and to recount stories. Setting aside the inaccuracy of this statement, the designs seen on the runways of Lagos, Dakar, or Johannesburg form a wide-open book in which tales of the past and of the future intermingle.

Above:
Maki Oh (brand
created by Amaka
Osakwe), details
of pieces from the
spring–summer 2017
collection, inspired by
Nigerian *aso-ebi* cloth.
© Emmanuelle Courrèges.

Facing page:
Maki Oh, looks from
the spring–summer
2017 collection.
© Kola Oshalusi/Insigna Media.

Jim Naughten, *Herero Woman in a Patterned Dress*, from the "Hereros" series, photographed in Namibia, 2012. © Jim Naughten.

TREND

Nº 6 Cº ANOMABU

Nº6COMP.

SAFOH

Kwamina Amoaku, *Asafo* flags made in the No. 6
Company, Anomabu, Ghana, c. 1970.

TREND

Facing page:
Karim Adduchi, look from the "She Knows Why the Caged Bird Sings" collection, spring–summer 2015, Amsterdam Fashion Week, July 2014.
© Team Peter Stigter.

Right:
Karim Adduchi, look from the "She Lives Behind the Courtyard Door" collection, spring–summer 2017, Amsterdam Fashion Week, July 2016.
© Team Peter Stigter.

I
n the seventeenth century, in what is today Ghana, two friends from the hunter caste came across a spider weaving its web. Based on their observations, they created the loom that is still used today to weave the renowned kente fabric. Nigerian fashion designer Bubu Ogisi took this legend from Ashanti oral tradition as one of the starting points for her I.AM.ISIGO spring–summer 2016 collection, entitled "Modern Hunters." On her mood board, next to photographs of weavers and men wearing *batakari*—short, wide masculine tunics made from woven bands of fabric—emerges a black-and-white depiction of the Ashanti queen Yaa Asantewaa who, in 1900, led a long battle against the British colonists in what came to be known as the War of the Golden Stool. "If you men will not go, then we women will do it. . . . We will fight until the last one of us falls on the battlefield," she allegedly declared. Inspired by the life of this historical icon, I.AM.ISIGO dresses and tunics—similar to the *batakari* the queen wore to disguise herself as a man—do much more than give body and substance to this epic. Bubu Ogisi, a master storyteller, uses myth to question her contemporaries through the use of bold colors like red or silver, metaphors for blood and metal; "shredded" finishes on dress hems; and traditional weaving blended with silk and viscose mesh borrowed from sportswear, to give modern silhouettes more of an athletic than bellicose appearance. "The most important part of this story, besides the queen's temerity in conducting the battle, is her courage," reveals the designer. "She was capable of guiding men, who showed little consideration for questions of gender, of leading them to battle to fight with her, for their land. My collection, inspired by men's clothing, traditionally worn and created by men, can be understood as a sign: that rules can be broken, and that women lose none of their power if they choose not to dress in an ostensibly feminine or sexy way."[1] Everything—from the *nwentoma* (the Ashanti word for woven garments) skillfully custom-made for I.AM.ISIGO in the Kumasi region of Ghana, to the vision and message—illuminates the social and political commitment of this new generation of fashion designers. Whether conjuring up the past and its shadows or questioning

TALES, HISTORY, AND REBELLIONS

the violence, paradoxes, stereotypes, and hypocrisy of the present, fashion becomes the vocabulary of contestation and a liberated space for designers where they can "document [their] truth," explains Faith Oluwajimi, founder of the label BLOKE. The female body, colonialism and apartheid, sexuality, Orientalism, human rights, violence toward women, migration and transhumance, new forms of masculinity: guided by African designers, a truly African voice rises to express the real, the singular, and the universal.

Like Bubu Ogisi, sisters Sylvia Enekwe-Ojei and Olivia Enekwe-Okoji of the Nigerian label Gozel Green question the boundaries of femininity. The female body is not "revealed" in their creations. Forms (breasts, buttocks) are barely emphasized and waists are not pronounced. In Ivory Coast, there is an ironic expression for provocative, sexy clothing intended to arouse (anytime and anywhere) male desire: the "I'm looking for a husband" dress. Gozel Green transforms women from being aesthetic objects of a gaze to subjects draped in narrative. "Our aim is to change the narrative around the way women 'should' dress and how they are perceived," declares Enekwe-Okoji. "We want the world to appreciate women for who they choose to be and not how they are expected to be. There's dignity in being yourself and staying true to yourself." Gozel Green's anti-conformist wardrobe

I.AM.ISIGO (brand created by Bubu Ogisi), dress from the "Modern Hunters" collection, spring–summer 2016, modeled by Uju Marshall. Art direction, hair, and makeup: Bubu Ogisi.
© Mambu Bayoh.

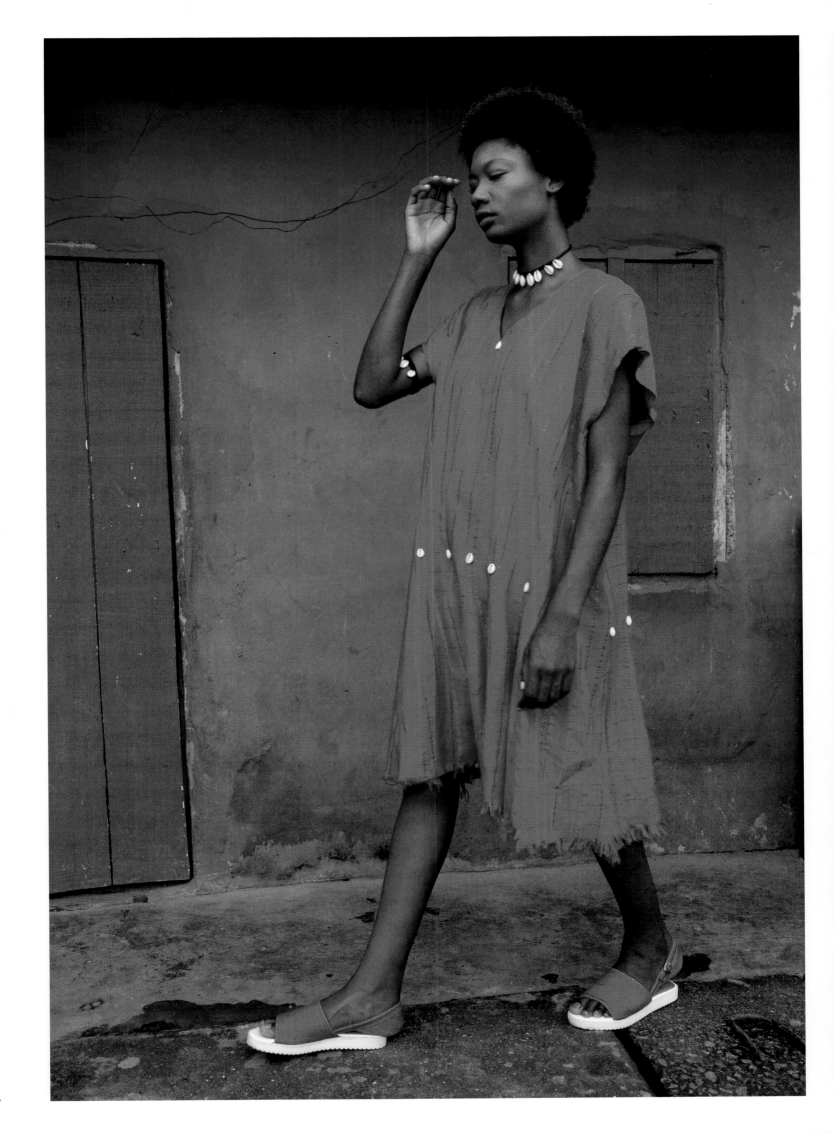

is "anti-stereotypes." In creating garments that give women freedom of movement and enable them to be dynamic, efficient, and visible through the interplay of materials, colors, and volumes, the Nigerian label also gives women a singular power—to own their strength without playing on or perverting it. These demands for freedom and the desire to smash the fetters of identity are echoed in the work of menswear designers such as BLOKE, Maxivive, Amine Bendriouich, and Orange Culture, to name just a few. Each in their own way is breaking with norms and changing the rules of the game. Skirts or dresses worn by men, transparent silk chiffon or organza blouses, lace pants: this is a generation with a deep-seated boldness. Amine Bendriouich remembers a lengthy debate with his mother about skirts, arguing that African wardrobes—Moroccan, in this case—were full of tunics, djellabas, caftans, harem pants, pagnes, dresses, and other blouses traditionally worn by men. "Both men and women wear djellabas and caftans. Why couldn't we also wear skirts?" he asks. "I wanted to wear certain female clothes, for example pleated skirts that resemble samurai garments. That was also a form of transgression. Clothing is just the accessory of attitude." This spirit of the skirt is found in his aptly named collection "A DNA"—as if to say that the unisex dimension running through it, as well as the Moroccan inflections and a tenderly indulgent imagination, are his signature. Orange Culture takes another approach to this quest for freedom—the freedom to be who we are or who we want to be. As a teenager, Adebayo Oke-Lawal, founder of the Nigerian label, suffered greatly from growing up in what he describes as a "hyper-masculine environment," where being different was frowned upon and asserting oneself was a dangerous enterprise. "That's why I built Orange Culture, to be more than a brand, and to be a movement that supports individuality and fights against stereotypes, against toxic masculinity," he explains. "I wanted to create clothing for people who felt different and wished to wear clothes that did more than just cover their nakedness; clothing that evoked emotion and told a story." He likes "fabric that feels vulnerable and evokes a feeling," as he makes clear in the vibrant colors and printed motifs interspersed throughout each of his

Below:
Gozel Green (brand created by Sylvia Enekwe-Ojei and Olivia Enekwe-Okoji), looks presented at Arise Fashion Week, Lagos, Nigeria, 2018.
© Kola Oshalusi/Insigna Media.

Facing page:
Amine Bendriouich, look from the "A DNA" collection, modeled by Hind Sahli, 2017.
© Mohcine Aoki.

collections. His world is one of sensuality, play, depth, and humor expressed in large flower-belts, quilted leather *agbada* (a kind of large boubou worn by men in Nigeria), knitted skirts (or pagnes) for men, beaded or rope plastrons, gold mustache-jewelry, and T-shirts printed with messages crying "Hear Me" or "See Me."

For many designers, fashion is a constantly renewed plea to respect human rights. "My goal is to use fashion to break down the walls built up around gender and self-expression," states Kenyan designer Eddy Patrick Muyishime of the label Muyishime. In one of his previous collections, he masterfully succeeded in creating ambiguity with a magnificent pair of trousers: with a high waist and darts, they would be considered "men's pants" if worn by a woman, but here, on a man, they take on a certain femininity, heightened by a pastel palette and crop top. Their fluidity pushes the boundaries of our ideas of gender. For his fall–winter 2021 collection, "Dear Sir/Madam (A Love Letter)," he says he was inspired by "the way people hide their true nature and their identity to blend into society, especially in Africa, where we have anti-LGBTQ laws. My intention was to show this, while still letting the colors shine to encourage people to be themselves." A canary-yellow petticoat peeks out from a trailing down-jacket dress, "marshmallow" sleeves reveal a white, barely hidden, diaphanous cape: this daring play of layers, the blend of urban and ultra-feminine, of technical fabrics and silk taffetas, and the sense of amused irony he brings to his use of traditionally "gendered" colors, together form an ensemble that is at once ambiguous and limpid, like a voice rising from the material to cry out a song of freedom.

With each new collection, South African designer Thebe Magugu celebrates the women of his country. The designer bears witness to their reality, suffering, courage, and struggles, whether drawing inspiration from tragic news stories that have shaken South Africa, like the murder of Karabo Mokoena by her boyfriend, or the Black Sash, a group of Black and white South African women who fought together against apartheid in the 1950s. In his fall 2018 collection, "Home Economics," the colors of his asymmetrical dresses and skirts, which resembled the packaging of housekeeping products, expressed the caustic nature of

Below:
Orange Culture (brand created by Adebayo Oke-Lawal), spring–summer 2016 collection, backstage at the runway show at Lagos Fashion Week, Nigeria, 2015.
© Emmanuelle Courrèges.

Facing page:
Ensemble from "The Flower Boy" collection, fall–winter 2020.
© Michael Oshai.

remarks women are likely to hear when they dare to assert themselves. But by dressing them in clean cuts, accented waists, and small corsets, he transformed them into poetic Amazons reclaiming their power. His compatriot Rich Mnisi also dedicates his creations to women—those in his family, in particular—demonstrating the richness of his own heritage. In his spring–summer 2021 collection, "Hiya Kaya," a "love letter" to the Tsonga people, vibrant prints and revisited *xibelani*[2] dance skirts celebrate his mother's power and fortitude, the vital energy that transcends history, and women's capacity for resilience—the women who make the transmission of History possible. And because he understands the dangers they face, despite the fire in their hearts, his sweaters bear the striking injunction "Protect Our Mothers."

This resilience is at the heart of South African designer Sindiso Khumalo's work. For her spring–summer 2020 collection, "Homecoming," she was inspired by the astonishing story of Sarah Forbes Bonetta, a young princess from the Dahomey kingdom (now Benin), who was abducted from her family in Nigeria. She escaped life as a slave when she was "gifted"[3] to Queen Victoria, becoming the queen's protégée.[4] Sindiso Khumalo has always been passionate about fabric and prints "because of their amazing power to evoke a mood or a feeling." She reinvents the world of Sarah's childhood by associating "Prairie"-style designs, gigot sleeves, high-necked and ruffled collars, and large hats fastened with ribbons—which would have been at home in her English wardrobe—with naive motifs representing the life of a young Zulu princess in a village in southern Africa.

Below: Muyishime (brand created by Eddy Patrick Muyishime), looks from the "Dear Sir/Madam (A Love Letter)" collection, fall–winter 2021. © Kelechi Amadi-Obi.

Facing page: Muyishime, "Pink Talash" suit, modeled by Deu Thiong, 2020. © Marvin Otieno.

That Sarah didn't grow up in South Africa is not the point; Sindiso Khumalo's tale is universal. Her collection brings the girl's intimate landscapes, like an indelible imprint, to the surface of the textiles—everything that she left behind when she arrived in Europe. "This wasn't the first time I'd worked with the idea of a character, but it was the first time I allowed her story to be an intrinsic part of my process," explains the designer. "I would dream about her, write about her, draw her. For me, producing collections isn't solely about making a beautiful product, it's also about going through some form of emotional and spiritual awakening." The humanity that Sindiso Khumalo confers on the girl in her collection resonates with the violence of past uprooting and contemporary migration, both dehumanizing forms of exile. In so doing, the printed tale releases its cathartic power and fashion becomes the universal healer.

Imane Ayissi also investigated history and its violence in 2009, in Rome, during Altaroma, and, ironically, during a show held in a convent where nuns planning to enter the Vatican are trained. His collection "Voodoo Mood" questioned the place of Black gods in a world where monotheism tried to smother them early on. With black and white to set the scene, little jackets covered in black or white quilted dolls, and dresses woven from vines like ritual cords, the designer restored texture, body, aura, and visibility to real, vibrant beliefs that had been forced underground. The pioneers paved the way by rehabilitating an African textile vocabulary; the time has now come for tales, for witness accounts, and for speaking out, in order to question, disrupt, and contribute to shaping a brighter tomorrow and to creating new communities of thought.

Pages 86–87:
Advertising campaign for Thebe Magugu's "ANTRHO 1" collection, fall–winter 2020.
© Travys Owen.

Left and above:
Rich Mnisi, looks from the "Hiya Kaya" collection, spring–summer 2021.
© Ricardo Simal.

Facing page:
Sindiso Khumalo, cotton dress from the spring–summer 2020 collection.
© Jonathan Kope.

"*Enviri* means 'hair' in Luganda, a language spoken by the Buganda people in Uganda. Each piece in this collection is symbolic of a woman's individual hair journey. The braided skirt, for example, evokes the deeply personal time when a girl has her hair braided by her mother, and the intimate and enriching relationship that develops through the conversations that take place during this task, which takes hours to complete. When designing and creating these pieces, I was conscious that they can and will be interpreted in many ways. However, they can also be said to have social and political implications. One could see this as a creative approach to advocacy."

Lamula Anderson
DESIGNER, ARTIST, AND FOUNDER OF THE BRAND LAMULA NASSUNA
@lamulanassuna

Lamula Nassuna,
dresses from
the "Enviri" collection,
fall–winter 2016.
© Othello De'Souza-Hartley.

Where but in Africa are the challenges of responsible fashion and the social and environmental questions raised by the production of clothing more relevant? While the West is concerned about economic losses from overproduction and unsold goods, and has recently begun to consider the industry's impact on humans and the environment, the African continent continues to receive a majority of textile waste produced in the Global North. Those used garments that don't end up in ponds and rivers, leeching toxic products into the water, or aren't incinerated, putting the health of local communities at risk, supply the secondhand clothing markets in Lomé, Abidjan, and Nairobi, affecting the entire textile industry. This situation, however, turns out to offer "creative material" for fashion designers. Some, like Nigerian designer Nkwo Onwuka and Senegalese designer Selly Raby Kane, use their collections to remind us that Africa, and certain lifestyles practiced there, constitute an inexhaustible yet extremely avant-garde source of inspiration.

For her spring–summer 2020 collection, "Be Us, Be Them," Nkwo Onwuka explains how she was inspired "by the way our ancestors lived in harmony with the earth. They took what they needed and put back the rest. They respected nature and one another. Today we live in societies that are technologically advanced but not very mindful of how much we produce or how much we consume, all in a bid to live more 'convenient' lifestyles. We can't go back to living exactly like our ancestors did, but we need to find the perfect balance between the way they lived then and the way we live now." The collection is crafted from *dakala*—a blend of cotton remnants woven in Funtua, in northeast Nigeria— and recycled denim, and created by Nkwo Onwuka herself (see p. 103). It is an ode to the many ethnic groups, including the Dassanech and Hamer, who populate the renowned Omo Valley in Ethiopia, and their fascinating ability to recycle elements of everyday life, such as bottle caps and SIM cards, into jewelry. The fabrics, cut

SUSTAINABLE, ETHICAL, AND ENVIRONMENTALLY RESPONSIBLE FASHION

up and sewn back together into strips, are also a metaphor for solar panels as "food for thought": a reminder of the resources present in our environments.

In many communities, recycling is a way of life. Selly Raby Kane has a unique talent for juxtaposing elements of Senegalese culture to form graphic puzzles. In her fall–winter 2017 collection, "17, rue Jules Ferry," she paid tribute to the sartorial tradition of the Baye Fall,[1] who depend on donations from their community, notably to make their clothes; their aesthetic is an extension of the spiritual message of austerity and humility that they embody. Several of Kane's dresses are imbued with the spirit of the Baye Fall *ndiakhass*[2] tunic, crafted from a patchwork of colorful fabric remnants that celebrate the possibility of "opulence obtained through frugality."[3] This tribute to "patchwork" and upcycling that preempts fashion draws heavily on cultures across Africa.

In Nairobi, Cape Town, Accra, Marrakech, and Lagos, each designer offers a singular interpretation of recycling that reflects his or her environment. In Kenya, which has one of Africa's largest markets for *mitumba* (secondhand clothing),

Selly Raby Kane, "Yoff" dress from the "17, rue Jules Ferry" collection, fall–winter 2017.
© Jean-Baptiste Joire.

Oliver Asike, founder of the festival Thrift Social Nairobi, created Vitimbi—a socially conscious line of clothes created using only secondhand pieces—because he couldn't find the clothing he wanted. He also wished to show that there is beauty to be found in secondhand clothes and textile waste: "the concept of making new from old fascinated me." The name Vitimbi comes from one of the most popular television shows in Kenya and means "intrigues" or "scheming" in Kiswahili. "Besides being a 'sustainable' brand, there are other layers to it, namely social and political commentary," explains the designer. Messages like "Corruption is evil" and "We care for Nairobians" are written on the backs of jackets. "As a native of a developing country, there are many problems that affect ordinary people, and I think that it is our responsibility to draw attention to these problems through fashion." For the last ten years, in Bamako's Missira district, Awa Meité has been creating bags woven from Malian cotton fibers and plastic thread from rice sacks processed by a local factory. Ivorian Loza Maléombho created several models for her spring–summer 2016 collection from hessian cut from cocoa sacks (Ivory Coast is the world's leading producer of cocoa) and dyed almond green. In South Africa, Marianne Fassler is a pioneer: while she rarely uses fabric as she finds it, she has insisted from her very first collection on reusing fabric from her stock by painting, beading, and shredding it. "I have a huge storeroom where every scrap is stored for future use. We have also often used discarded secondhand jeans, sweaters, coats, and garments sourced on the streets of Johannesburg, where huge bales of discarded clothes are dumped. Because of this practice, small tailors and workshops practicing traditional tailoring in Africa are unable to sustain themselves in this kind of market. These acts of so-called charity are not welcome. . . . My use of these pieces is always a sociopolitical comment." Similarly, the Ghanaian label Studio One Eighty Nine and Cameroonian designer Imane Ayissi regularly use their own fabric remnants to create patchwork jeans of woven indigo or haute couture dresses with a social message. In 2021, Ivory Coast label Laurence Airline took a similar approach for the launch of the capsule collection "Children of the Earth," created entirely from upcycled former collections and dedicated to nature and protecting the forests.

Other African designers, like Faith Oluwajimi of BLOKE, source fabric from stockists or suppliers that offer vintage fabric, in some cases from major international fashion houses. In the heart of Marrakech, in an Aladdin's cave run by a nearly hundred-year-old enthusiast, Amine Bendriouich unearthed treasures including Yves Saint Laurent's first leopard prints, Japanese silk velvet, cottons from previous Donna Karan collections, and extraordinary materials from French stockist Abraham. These finds inspired collections like "Winter in Africa" (2013) and "Gnawa Bombs" (2016). This sourcing choice may imply designing one-of-a-kind or limited-edition pieces, such as those created by South African designer Lezanne Viviers for her eponymous label. "Because we aim to minimize textile waste, we produce limited-edition runs that avoid the production of dead stock. When we aren't creating our own textiles, we make use of dead stock fabrics we find in South African warehouses, closed since the 1970s and '80s, that sport immaculate quality of a kind that existed before the era of mass production."

Secondhand clothes flood the entire continent. Some designers, such as Amah Ayivi for the label Marché Noir, bring them back to Europe in a back-and-forth exchange that is both ironic and valuable, accomplishing the considerable feat of transforming them into works of art. By blending a silk kimono found in a flea market, a knitted doily, metallic fabric, a vintage Moroccan *handira* blanket, or an antique jabot shirt with traditional African garments, brocades, North African beadwork, or Hausa embroidery, Artsi Ifrach, founder of the Moroccan label ART/C (see pp. 2–3 and 110–11), creates a dazzling intercultural symphony, proving that art is indeed the antidote to death—and that nothing beats this mash-up and the sensations it arouses to create a "new lease of life" for clothing. For his spring–summer 2020 capsule collection, "Regenerated Lola," Papa Oyeyemi, founder of the Nigerian brand Maxivive, pushes the envelope even further: the six pieces in the collection are designed entirely from a stock of printed scarves bearing

Maxivive (brand founded by Papa Oyeyemi), look from the "Regenerated Lola" shirt collection, 2020, modeled by Blessing.
© Walter Banks.

the logo of the famous international brand that discarded them. Upcycling, coupled with "reclaiming" the brand name—also incorporated into the collection title—becomes a manifesto: "There are too many garments in the world, we don't have to make new ones from scratch anymore. We can easily recycle and upcycle a whole lot more," claims the designer.

The Kenyan brand Asha : Eleven, launched in 2018 and one of the most sustainable in Africa, chose to limit its environmental impact by opting for digital printing. Others, such as Studio One Eighty Nine, have, on the contrary, attempted to "clean up" traditional handicraft techniques that have often been corrupted and altered by modern practices. In textiles, as in other fields like architecture and construction, changes in lifestyle have influenced the choice to use more chemical products that speed up the production process. Leading textile design artists, including Malian Aboubakar Fofana and Nigerian Nike Okundaye, Boubacar Doumbia's group Kasobané, and the Ndomo initiative have demonstrated that it is possible—in the case of indigo, *adire*, *bogolan*, and other fabrics—to reverse this trend by creating textiles according to original "good practices," which turn the fabrication process into an added value. A few designers have also chosen to work with organic raw materials, such as organic Faso Dan Fani—the emblematic fabric of Burkina Faso—used by Imane Ayissi in his spring–summer 2020 collection, "Akouma." Fashion designer Awa Meité works with nearly 150 women organic cotton farmers in Shô, about ten miles from Bamako. There, she has created a production center where cotton—"white gold"—is given added value. Though Mali is the leading African producer of the fiber, the country still processes too little of it; to optimize the harvest and offer sustainable possibilities for the region, about a dozen women were trained and are now responsible for spinning thread and weaving. Developed with respect for local lifestyles and production methods, the program has encouraged others like it. "Working with the weavers is not only more environmentally friendly than several of our other handicrafts, it is versatile and seems to be a great way to empower women," asserts Nkwo Onwuka, who has

worked extensively with *aso-oke* weavers in Nigeria's Kogi state. Kenneth Ize, I.AM. ISIGO, Nourredine Amir, Sindiso Khumalo, Emmy Kasbit, Maki Oh: whether they have created their own workshops or collaborate occasionally with a cooperative or artisan collective, they all contribute to developing a human-centered industry that increases employment opportunities, while helping to preserve ancestral know-how. Although industry enables high-volume production and the Internet connects the world, everyone knows that only slow fashion—fashion that unites the human, craftsmanship, and respect for lifestyles and the environment—can, in the coming decades, protect humanity and cultures. Here, time does not equal money; it is the lifeblood of a better tomorrow.

Facing page:
Anyango Mpinga,
dress from the
"Phonology"
collection, spring–
summer 2019, Lagos
Fashion Week,
Nigeria, 2018.
© Kola Oshalusi/Insigna Media.

Above:
Asha : Eleven
(brand created by
Olivia Kennaway),
"Maridadi" ensemble,
modeled by Akual
Chan, 2021. Makeup:
Duki Styling.
© Rogers Ouma (M. Ojwook).

Page 98:
Lara Klawikowski,
"Ficus Elastica"
dress in recycled,
biodegradable plastic,
from the "Strange
Flowers" collection,
spring–summer 2020,
modeled by Olivia
Sang (Boss Models
Cape Town) for the
online magazine
Africa Is Now.
© Michael Oliver Love.

Page 99:
Laurence Airline,
suit in hand-
decorated, woven
pagne cloth, from the
"Children of the Earth"
collection, modeled
by David J. Kabamba,
2021.
© Trevor Stuurman.

Looks and accessories
by the sustainable
Kenyan brand
Vitimbi (created
by Oliver Asike).
Courtesy Vitimbi
Clothing Brand.

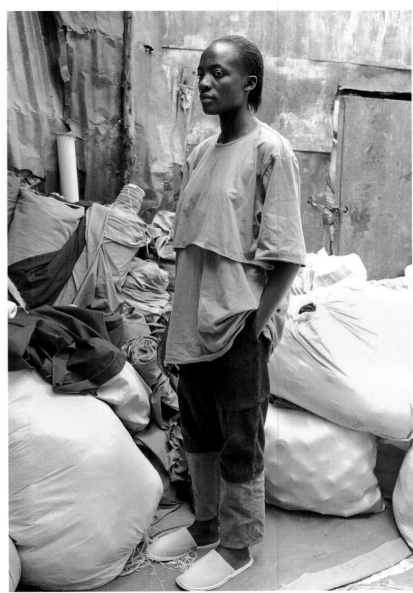

TRADITION

A young Dassanech girl in Omorate, Omo Valley, Ethiopia, 2011. © Georges Courrèges.

TREND

TRADITION

Weaver in designer Awa Meité's weaving workshop
in the Missira district of Bamako, Mali, 2011.

TREND

FOCUS

ACCESSORIES ◆

Accessories provide the perfect opportunity for African craft skills and expertise to shine. Lending prestige to the continent's raw materials or revisiting traditional forms and patterns, jewelry, shoes, and bags created by talented designers are the best ambassadors for African cultures.

A goat hide—the *maroquin*—imported from Morocco to Europe in the late sixteenth century and produced using a sumac-based African tanning technique, gave rise to the French word for leather goods, *maroquinerie*. It is no surprise that many brands use leather, whether sourced from Ethiopia, Morocco, South Africa, or Egypt. Contemporary fashion designers offer a vast and varied repertory of designs inspired by the goldwork of the Akan people of Ghana and Ivory Coast; the sophisticated silverwork of the Berber and Tuareg tribes; Maasai forms and beadwork; Hausa embroideries; Xhosa or Zulu beadwork; Yakuba ritual headdresses covered in cowry shells; and Rwandan Imigongo art.

Bags by Okhtein celebrate exquisite brasswork and Egyptian craft skills; sandals by Ifele, crafted in collaboration with a cooperative of women experts in beaded leather from KwaZulu-Natal, revisit traditional Zulu *izimbadada* footwear; *babouche* slippers by footwear brand Zyne infuse traditional Moroccan passementerie with edgy or romantic touches; bags by AAKS showcase basketwork from Bolgatanga, Ghana; Hamethop accessories pay tribute to the creativity of Ndebele women; and footwear by Goya combines leather with cloth woven by Senegalese Manjak weavers. Whether simplifying the ostentatious or refining a process, many brands endeavor to work with local artisans. Others practice upcycling: Reform Studio in Egypt and Miswude in Senegal use recycled plastics and remnants of leather and cloth, respectively. Ready-to-wear brands also offer lines of bags and jewelry, such as tote bags by Thebe Magugu and sandals by Loza Maléombho embellished with miniature Dan masks from Ivory Coast.

Kayadua (brand created by Eyiwaa Agyekumhene), cotton macramé necklace-plastron, 2020.
© Bernard Nana Appiah/ Fodoa Photos.

1

5

1
Pichulik (brand created by Katherine-Mary Pichulik), "Cantadora" earrings from the "Magi" collection, fall–winter 2020, modeled by Zomassa Gneki. Hair and makeup: Amori Birch.
© Alix-Rose Cowie.

2
Ifele (brand created by Reggi Xaba), sandals inspired by traditional Zulu *izimbadada*.
Courtesy Ifele.

3
Goya Paris (brand created by Rodrigue Vodonou), ankle boots in leather and woven pagne cloth, 2019.
Courtesy Goya Paris.

4
Rokus London (brand created by Marie-Paule Tano), "Half Moon" earrings, photograph published in *Nikkou* magazine, 2020.
© 2020 by Sam Ssefa.

5
Ami Doshi Shah, polished brass necklaces made from ethical, sustainable materials, from the "Salt of the Earth" collection, 2020.
© Maganga Mwagogo.
Courtesy Ami Doshi Shah.

4

2

3

7

6
Shekudo (artistic director: Akudo Iheakanwa), "Nwadi" and "Nkiru" bags from the "Series 1: Woven Ties" collection, 2019.
Courtesy Shekudo.

7
Hamethop (brand created by Tsakani Mashaba), beaded bag featuring patterns inspired by the Ndebele people.
Courtesy Hamethop.

8
Okhtein (brand created by Aya and Mounaz Abdel Raouf), "Minat" clutch in crocodile-print leather, 2020.
Courtesy Okhtein.

9
Adèle Dejak jewelry and Johanna Bramble headscarf, modeled by Shanelle Nyasiase.
© Adèle Dejak.

8

9

Leather and gilt bronze sandal belonging to the king of Bonoua, Abouré, Ivory Coast, 1985.

Sandals created by Loza Maléombho, backstage at Lagos Fashion Week, Nigeria, October 2016. © Sylvain Cherkaoui/Cosmos.

TREND

Young dancers wearing cowrie headdresses, Ivory Coast, photograph by Michael Kirtley, published in National Geographic (vol. 160, no. 1, July 1982)

TREND

African or not African? The debate regularly pits those who believe that wax is above all an import, evidence of colonialist economic expansion and detrimental to traditional African craft skills, against those who, on the contrary, see it as a fabric "belonging to Africa." A signature fabric, wax print is clearly part of the collective unconscious. It also seems to summarize—metaphorically—the North's perception of the African continent as a single place with a single language. Beyond obscuring the immense variety of African textiles, this injurious perception prevents the diversity of contemporary African fashion creations from being imagined or represented. Among the designers who present at Africa's major fashion weeks (Lagos, Johannesburg, Cape Town, Dakar, Addis-Ababa, Kigali), very few use this fabric and only a small number, such as Nigerian designer Lisa Folawiyo, have managed to imbue it with a distinctive spirit. Her dresses made of *ankara* (the name given to wax prints in Nigeria), featuring patterns embroidered with fine beadwork, have built her reputation. Her compatriot Ituen Basi has also succeeded in bringing a healthy dose of ingenuity to these all too familiar prints. In South Africa, designer Palesa Mokubung's label Mantsho uses *shweshwe*: a cotton fabric imported by the English, blended with silk or linen. In Zanzibar, off the east coast of Africa, Doreen Mashika introduced *kanga* (also called *lesso* or *leso*) to ready-to-wear; her dress collections revisit this cotton fabric printed with proverbs or phrases, traditionally worn by women as pareus or headscarves. Wax prints have also inspired several brands created by the African diaspora, such as Ray Darten in the United States. In France, Maison Château-Rouge and By Natacha Baco have risen to the challenge of giving this fabric a contemporary twist.

Wax fabric, named for the wax-printing process (called "resist printing"), takes its inspiration from traditional Indonesian batik fabric. In the mid-nineteenth century, the Dutch, in the midst of colonial expansion, developed an industrial process to manufacture the cloth. The Ashanti people of Ghana[1]—recruited by the Dutch to assist in conquering the island of Java—showed such enthusiasm for the fabric that the Europeans decided to produce it for sale on the continent. Africa's printed fabrics are like the pages of a history book: they tell of colonialist opportunism and its methods, but they also recount the intelligence shown by African peoples, to this day, to get around deceitful tactics and use language to appropriate fabrics and their patterns. When, to increase the fabric's popularity, the Dutch began to market patterns inspired by African cultures and motifs, such as a fly swatter or a stool, Africans quickly renamed the pagnes after their local proverbs. A design featuring the royal *akan* stool, for example, became in everyday Ghanaian language the pagne "If you want to tell me something, sit down and say it to my face." The famous Nana Benz of Togo[2] contributed heavily to this phenomenon. What makes wax-print fabric African is this rechristening, distancing, reappropriation, and repurposing of the medium, undertaken by Africans themselves.

Ituen Basi, runway show presenting the "Balogun" collection, spring–summer 2020, at GTBank Fashion Weekend, November 2019.
© Kola Oshalusi/Insigna Media.

Abrima Erwiah

COFOUNDER, WITH ROSARIO DAWSON, OF STUDIO ONE EIGHTY NINE @studiooneeightynine

" It is in Africa that I became aware of the intimate bond that connects us, humans, to our environment, to nature, animals, and trees. No element can survive without the others. I think it's wonderful, the chain that exists between plants, food, and, for example, textile dyeing: onions, avocados, beets—each one contributes to creating natural dyes that respect the environment. Africa is a pioneering continent when it comes to recycling; nothing is wasted and everything is transformed. Upcycling isn't a trend; it's a way of life. With the increasing demand for indigo-dyed fabric, and in order to reduce production times, chemical products have begun to be used in some countries. We work in Mali, Burkina Faso, and Ghana, with communities that follow good practices and meet criteria respectful of humans and the environment. When some of the craftspeople with whom we regularly worked didn't know where the products they were using came from, we analyzed the textiles in a laboratory; now the entire production chain is local, ethical, and sustainable, from the cotton to the dyes. Today, we must all create with the concept of 'circularity' in mind—the idea that we are responsible for what we produce from beginning to end.

Sending used clothes to Africa is not the solution. Especially considering that, while some people do this out of 'charity,' the clothes aren't free as, in reality, they are sold, not given. But more importantly, a world that consumes more and more clothes each year means we're going to send more containers without providing the people receiving them with the means for responsible management. On site, the secondhand clothes that haven't been sold wind up abandoned; they end up in the water, where the chemical products seep out. Africa is not a trash can. Even if this trade benefits certain vulnerable populations, there are other ways to create jobs. "

Rosario Dawson (left) and Abrima Erwiah (right).
© Joshua Jordan.
Courtesy of Studio189.

Marrakech, 2018.
© Suzana Holtgrave.

Artsi Ifrach

FOUNDER OF MAISON ART/C @maisonartc

" Rather than 'African fashion,' I always prefer to talk about culture. I think that Africa and African fashion designers relate to culture in such a profound way that it is practically in their DNA. It is this dynamism, this vibrant side that challenges people. When you go to Europe—to Paris, Milan, London—it's roughly the same brands, the same kind of food everywhere. Western brands do not have this kind of DNA, as their approach to fashion is more commercial than cultural. Culture is our added value, and nothing inspires me more than the dialogue that can be established between each of our cultures.

I travel all over the world—in Nigeria, Ethiopia, Asia—and I visit a lot of markets everywhere. The art of the street is the liveliest. I like nothing better than to see the time and dedication people give to creative work, to craftsmanship. In the North, everything is structured, very comfortable. In Africa, the lack of that comfort pushes people to be more creative. I'm very mindful of the way the clothes are made, what they symbolize, and the human value behind them. I think that, by doing this, the first things I provoke through my work are emotions and memories, which allow you to look at the garments, the culture, and the beauty of it all with a certain respect. In my shop, people buy stories. And while many people would always like to dress 'new' or be 'new' themselves, for me, the future is actually to go backwards. Drawing from what already exists: a piece of clothing, a unique piece. . . . Take the caftan, for example. It's like a kimono for me; I'm trying to show how precious it is. My fashion is an opinion: it deals with politics, religion, and social issues. "

Makeup: Odiri Dit It.
© Chidi "Lex Ash" Ashimole.

Reni Folawiyo

**FOUNDER AND CEO OF ALARA,
CONCEPT STORE, LAGOS, NIGERIA** @alaralagos

> More than a particular aesthetic, what African fashion designers have in common today—this idea of 'Africanness'—is the sense of belonging based on similar experiences. Reaffirming our ownership and use of our own culture and techniques is important, but in the end it's what we do with them that will make our designers stand out. Designers have such a huge wealth of stories to tell!

Many creators are starting to learn the value of their heritage which, with its notion of traditions, know-how, and handmade craftsmanship, corresponds to the international definition of luxury. This is why it's important to preserve traditional skills and make Africans a force in the luxury field. You have Kenneth Ize, whose world is based almost exclusively on handmade methods, which he is constantly refining and upgrading, to create beautiful contemporary pieces, of course, but also to preserve the skills of the artisans he works with. When I think of African luxury, this is what I think of: the invaluable connection to and 'uplifting' of the maker—the fact that an object you paid good money for will not only bring great joy, but has uplifted and will continue to uplift an artisan.

Africa, like the rest of the world, is concerned with contemporary discussions. The greatness of African creators lies in the promise and the uniqueness of their message, the hugely untapped potential in traditional methods, the talent of Africa's youth, and the exceptional potential for innovation based on our history, our tenacity, and our inventiveness. Connecting this globally-aware youth to its roots is going to be tremendous. This African cultural renaissance, the ultimate realization of one's own value and the desire to own one's narrative—this was always going to happen. The beauty of seeing it all come together, a celebration and acknowledgement of our own excellence, is so exciting. **"**

Imane Ayissi

COUTURIER @imane_ayissi

"When working with African textiles, an important question arises: 'To what degree can they be altered?' A balance must be struck between tradition and innovation. For the 2021-22 fall-winter collection "Madzang," I created a coat using kente cloth made from merino wool. The design, which hadn't worked at all in baby alpaca, proved magnificent in this type of woolen material. Working in this way, it is possible to modify composition, color, and weight by weaving threads one by one instead of two by two, in order to make a lighter weft, for example. I like to 'shake things up,' in a way, so at times I've expanded the repertoire of designs, the ideograms found on certain traditional textiles. Sometimes the weavers look at me like I'm crazy, but they're also amused; I think they enjoy working this way.

Together, we redraw the boundaries of fashion. And although the weavers have to adjust their way of working, their creative input is still essential. There are always surprises when the strips of fabric arrive at the atelier: the weavers are given instructions, along with the choice of threads and colors, but they follow their own inspiration. And when I put the strips together, it isn't always in the way they imagined I would. It's a dance we perform together that requires each of us to contribute a bit of ourselves. For international consumers, this world is unlikely to be perceived as a luxury sector, but to me, it is the very essence of luxury. I like preserving the imperfections in the fabrics and bringing out the thickness of the seams. The mark of the maker infuses a garment with life."

Around the world, clothing is seen as a marker of social and cultural identity. It tells others who we are, where we live—and sometimes who we want to be.

Like the catwalks of Lagos, Dakar, and Johannesburg, where astounding creativity is on display, the streets of Africa are also brimming with styles as diverse as they are astonishingly bold. Fashion is a narrative experience, and while photography has existed in Africa since the late nineteenth century, attesting to a fondness for self-representation (especially in the work of West Africa's great portrait photographers of the 1950s to 1970s, Seydou Keïta, Mama Casset, and Malick Sidibé), the emergence of social media and the arrival on the continent of smartphones has intensified the phenomenon. Outside the confines of the photographer's studio, a whole generation of liberated youth combines performance, story, and fantasy to create a new visual narrative for Africa.

Times have changed: in societies where group culture traditionally dictated customs and appearances, individuals, liberated from exclusive structures of belonging, now dare to assert their originality. Published on blogs and on Instagram, images of a street style that flamboyantly combines reflection and spontaneity—an unlikely juxtaposition befitting these exercises in style—also form a manifesto for re-enchanting a reality that has been deformed, caricatured, or rendered static by the Western lens. "And what better way to do this than to participate in the visual economy of fashion, which has been so deeply complicit in spreading these twisted epistemologies," observes Italian researcher Enrica Picarelli.[1] "We tell our own stories with our fabrics, our fashion, and our African signs and symbols," says Emmanuel Ekuban, founder of @Debonairafrik, an online platform and one of the most followed Instagram accounts dedicated to African fashion. "Each image we share contains a fragment of Africa, our Africa, as we see it." To Enrica Picarelli, who invented the term "Afrosartorialists" in 2014, this generation is above all a generation of powerful storytellers. "Interestingly, the brand of the garments is not usually mentioned, unless these are works for specific designers. But even in that case, the human and lived aspects of the performance take up more space than the mere advertising of the clothes," she explains. And the story resonates: no matter how appealing an image may be, the comments left by followers more often relate to the message being conveyed than the garments themselves. "Look into the future and mark where you belong," intones Kenyan visual artist Moh McKenzie in a comment on Instagram, where his slogan is "Turning Everyday Objects into Stylish Accessories." He and his associate, Clint Malik, master the art of reappropriation, gleaning material from their surroundings to feed their aesthetic approach. "Using everyday objects and old relics that are often misperceived is not only the cheapest and most mind-blowing way of creating artsy futuristic fashion accessories and giving meaning to things that were seen as trash; it also shows and teaches my community and the world the importance of being unique. It's a way of showing them that nothing is impossible and that being different is attractive." They use matches, paper clips, aluminum foil, fragments of shattered mirrors, and parts from tools or machines found in the junkyard to create striking customized shirts, glasses, and blazers.

Their jeans, painted tongue-in-cheek with the words "made in Kenya," speak volumes about the extraordinary art of recycling, mastered by so many of Africa's talented designers. In their case, "recycling" is synonymous with appropriating and transforming pieces, some sourced from elsewhere, using reflection, humor, and an innate sense for repositioning meaning. In choosing alternative tools to tell their story, by overlapping urban and traditional wardrobes, or by, for example, pairing a designer suit with a tajine dish as a hat, these designers assert their vision of style and define the lens through which they observe their environment. In the process, Moh McKenzie and other artists—such as Moroccans Karim Chater (alias @stylebeldi) and Zineb Koutten, the Kenyan creative collective @2manysiblings, created by Velma Rossa and Oliver Asike, or the late Louis Philippe de Gagoue at the beginning of his career—challenge traditional fashion codes. While some see eschewing the brand system (including African brands) as a step away from fashion, or even an admission of insufficient purchasing power, for others it is proof of independence from diktats handed down from on high. It is a lesson in freedom—or emancipation. Pieces discovered in the flea markets of Nairobi, Casablanca, Lomé,

and Bamako, removed from the fashion apparatus that sanctified them, achieve new status: their value is restored through the creative intentions of designers and fashionistas, who render them truly African by using them as tools to reassert control over their image. Art always offers a new beginning.

Although Oliver Asike (also founder of the brand Vitimbi, see pp. 100–101) did not create the festival Thrift Social for political reasons, but rather from a desire to "bring Nairobi's various fashion tribes—skaters, hippies, style bloggers, fashionistas—into one space to connect and grow the Kenyan creative scene," he nevertheless organized the event with sustainable living in mind. In addition to hosting a number of music groups, this three-day fashion and music festival, which has become one of the most influential in East Africa, welcomes secondhand labels and brands that practice recycling. "It's an extension of my personal style, which has been influenced in a major way by secondhand clothing. A lot of young guys in Nairobi are into secondhand clothing as a means of sustainable living, both financially and environmentally," he explains. Fashion provides a way to sublimate reality—in every sense of the word.

Below:
Louis Philippe
de Gagoue
in Bouznika,
Morocco, 2014.
© Déborah Benzaquen.

Facing page:
Louis Philippe
de Gagoue.
© Raphaël Liais.

"Basically, I began wearing the hijab because I didn't like my hair. And then I fell in love with this new identity. It truly expresses who I am. I like classic pieces and 'modest' fashion, but I've always wanted to be different. There are many things that distract us from the reality of beauty, and we often give value to things that don't deserve it. Through my looks, I want people to know that they can create their own style and be fashionable with secondhand clothes. That's something I truly believe."

Zineb Koutten
VLOGGER AND ARTIST
@zineb_koutten_

Clockwise,
from top left:

Campaign for
the 2021 Fashion
Trust Arabia Prize,
Casablanca,
Morocco, 2020.
Zineb Koutten is
wearing a jacket
by Aybee.
© Joseph Ouechen.

Koutten
photographed by one
of her sisters, 2019.

Koutten
photographed
by @adamhgrey,
2020.

Koutten
photographed
by Karim Chater
(Style Beldi), 2020.

Fashion subcultures are always an expression of resistance, such as the joyful vengeance of the legendary Congolese *sapeurs*.[2] In another act of social sublimation, they "borrow" their suits, fedoras, and canes from European sartorialists, injecting a dose of color in dazzling revenge against the former colonists whose dark clothes matched their dark methods. Creating or belonging to a "fashion tribe" when one lives in Bacongo, a neighborhood in Brazzaville, or in a township in South Africa, is to symbolically cast off the role or position imposed by a system. It is an attempt to avoid classification, whatever it may be, by creating a "patchwork identity": a quilt of lived experience, preferences, and perspectives. It is also—as was the case in South Africa in the aftermath of Apartheid—a manifesto for the freedom to be oneself, as illustrated by the series "Beauty Is in the Eye of the Beholder" (see pp. 145 and 188), created in 2003 in Cape Town by South African photographer Nontsikelelo Veleko, or by the members of the Smarteez collective, who create looks that combine dandy spirit with Soweto culture. South African fashion editor Asanda Sizani describes them as being exactly what was needed in a country where communities had been given so little opportunity to express themselves and to be who they wanted to be.[3] Fashion is a loom with which to weave dreams and restitch the world. Some creatives, unable to afford their dream garments—like young "Salah Versace," who proudly bears the Italian brand's logo tattooed on his head—demonstrate their incredible ability to work with and appropriate elements from the system with an ingenuity that, in many cases, far exceeds the original. Others dare to be themselves in defined spaces. "While walking around Casablanca, I photographed two young men I saw arrive in the city center, then pull out their sunglasses from their pockets, along with colorful scarves and bucket hats, and put them on. They clearly enjoyed being different, but they couldn't do so in their own neighborhood," recounts Moroccan photographer Joseph Ouechen. Throughout Africa—but also in New York, London, and Paris—music festivals and urban events provide a setting where participants are free to express

Above:
No Couscous,
Casablanca,
Morocco, 2018.
© Joseph Ouechen.

Right:
Salah Versace,
Casablanca,
Morocco, 2017.
© Joseph Ouechen.

Facing page:
Karim Chater
(Style Beldi).
© Mohcine Harisse.

their personal style. In Casablanca, the alternative festival L'Boulevard[4] provides a safe place to proudly display one's culture and cast off the straitjacket of social conventions, whether in a total punk look with mohawk, studded jacket, and a T-shirt bearing political messages, or in a soccer jersey—the "signature" garment worn by Berber shopkeepers—covered with slogans in Amazigh.[5] "The festival says a lot about us as Moroccans," explains Ouechen, "about where we want to go and about our quest for freedom. For three days, the space supports an entire generation and allows it to simply exist." Ouechen practices what he calls "No Couscous" photography: in other words, an approach devoid of stereotypes; he enjoys documenting transformations and capturing the voices that emerge from this experimentation. "I like it when people use what they have, when there's a depth and a demand conveyed with a look. A young man who dyes his hair purple is redefining masculinity in Morocco," he says. Every year since 2011, the urban festival Chale Wote, held in Accra's historic Jamestown neighborhood, has been the setting for a popular, art-infused procession where clothing takes center stage on every street corner. Founded by the cultural platform Accra[dot]Alt to raise awareness among communities about contemporary artistic creation in fields as varied as dance, fine arts, graffiti, and film, the opening day has morphed into a huge, weeklong celebration that now welcomes more than thirty thousand people from around the world each year. Meaning "Let's go, my friend" in the Ga language,[6] Chale Wote, in addition to many artistic events, offers a collective street experience where everyone gathers to make a statement or express pride in belonging—primarily through their appearance. Artists, performers, and ordinary participants transform the parade into a joyful display of freedom of expression in wildly diverse attire—from a dress-cloak fashioned from an LGBT flag, or an outfit made of recycled plastic condemning the material's devastating environmental effects, to looks incorporating traditional body paint, a half-woman half-man costume, and tunics made from Malian *bogolan* cloth paired with Mossi necklaces from Burkina-Faso and funky glasses.

In Kinshasa, in the Democratic Republic of the Congo, both self-taught and academically trained artists decked out in secondhand clothes, soda cans, car parts, and flip-flop soles embody figures that decry the wrongs of society. Their powerful spirit of dissent is felt in their use of masks, the ultimate messenger in many traditional societies and a highly creative and ultra-visual means of expression. Whether walking the catwalk at Kinact—an urban festival created by Kinshasa-based artist Eddy Ekete—or creating one-off street performances, Congolese artists use "style" and appearance as formidable tools of protest in the fight against pollution,

Above:
Collaboration
between Christian
Kamgaing
(@makchris_,
photographer) and
Yvanna "Shooter"
Abena (art director),
clothing modeled
by Loïc Abondo
and Manuel Karim,
Yaoundé, Cameroon,
2020.
© Christian Kamgaing.

Facing page:
TSAU—The Space
Around Us (brand
created by Bevan
Agyemang).

poverty, and waste from the West that has turned "*Kin la plus belle* (Kin the most beautiful)" into "*Kin la poubelle* (Kin the trash can)," to quote local inhabitants, as well as to condemn the damaging impact of the cellphone industry.[7] For the magazine *Off To,*[8] photographer Prisca Monnier captured the magnetic force of Bakeli collective member Junior Mvunzi, whose sculptural work *Mabele Y'a Mboka* (which means "land of our country," or for Mvunzi, "land of our ancestors") seems otherworldly, with its metal wings created entirely from scrapped electronic components manufactured using the red copper and aluminum that make up the Congolese soil. The work criticizes the country's impoverishment by foreign multinationals, despite its immense resources. This Afrofuturist angel carries the message of another possible future. "I salvaged our raw material from old telephones and computers to create beauty. It's a way of showing the world that nothing can stop us, that it is possible to find a balance for all."[9]

Similar metamorphoses can be observed from one end of Africa to the other in the increasing efforts to renew and valorize African cultural heritage. In Abidjan, designer Lafalaise Dion gained recognition by creating headdresses from cowrie shells, inspired by those worn by

Below, left:
Kamal, Marrakech, Morocco, 2020.
© Joseph Ouechen.

Below, right:
Photograph published in the online magazine *A Nasty Boy*, 2019.
Styling: Moses Ebite.
© Michael Oshai.

Facing page:
Sibu VI, from the "Beauty Is in the Eye of the Beholder" series, 2003–6.
©Nontsikelelo Veleko.

the Yacouba people in western Ivory Coast, which she pairs with ultra-modern looks. "I see them much more as crowns than as fashion accessories," says the artist. "Like many young people of my generation, I was separated from my original culture and its spirituality. I wanted to reappropriate my history and display my heritage." She created the headdresses following extensive conversations with the elders of her family village, and appeared in one for the first time at the Chale Wote festival in Accra, where it met with immediate success. "Everyone wanted to try it on and have one of their own. I realized that I shared the same desire and the same approach with Africans of my generation." And although she had not considered selling her decorative headdresses, orders have begun pouring in from around the world, from South Africa to the United States. The tiny shell has such evocative power that in her music video "Spirit," Beyoncé wears one of Dion's creations: a sensual, mystical cowrie veil.

In Dakar, Khadija Aisha Ba, creator of the brand L'Artisane[10] and the label and boutique Le Sandaga,[11] also wears her heritage with pride. She discovered her passion for Senegalese boubous—which she modernizes with bold pairings, like Converse sneakers—in the wardrobe of her grandfather, Sidy Alpha Ba. Khadija Aisha Ba has always been fascinated by the voluminous nature of these garments, staples of traditional wardrobes in Senegal and throughout West Africa. She loves them for their comfort and noble appearance, and infuses them with her own puckish spirit, cutting boubous from camouflage fabric and embroidering hamburger designs on sumptuous *bazin* cloth.

Along with this movement to restore value and "recast" African textile, sartorial, and cultural heritage, which unites an entire generation, boundaries have blurred. A sense of belonging has developed that reaches beyond nationality: these shared wardrobes embody the dream of Pan-Africanism.[12] South African visual artist and influencer Trevor Stuurman feels, in his own words, "royal" when wearing L'Artisane boubous. "Instagram has become a sort of visual university where young Africans can discover what is happening in other countries in Africa and draw inspiration from them," observes Emmanuel Ekuban. Throughout the continent—and among its diasporas—ancestral hairstyles are experiencing a genuine revival. Nigerian singer Falana draws inspiration from styles worn by the Himba people of Namibia; South African influencer Kwena Baloyi, from ancient headdresses worn by Peul women; and Kenyan actress Lupita Nyong'o, from Amasunzu, an elaborate Rwandan hairstyle. Many Instagram accounts such as @thekraal, @afrodyssee, and @ancestrallife are genuine treasure troves, overflowing with inspirational archival photos. The most cutting-edge women share images by Nigerian photographer J.D.'Okhai Ojeikere, whose work on Nigerian hairstyles has been exhibited around the world and continues to inspire many photographers. Franco-Congolese celebrity hairstylist Nadeen Mateky has brought vintage back into fashion with a creative approach inspired by African kings and queens, prophetesses, and iconic African figures of resistance, such as Kimpa Vita.[13] "The hairstyles from these eras were very sophisticated and very technical," she explains. "I don't copy them exactly; I add volume, height, ornamentation, Baoulé weights,[14] Tukulor jewelry,[15] or Nigerian pearls that I bring back from my travels. Ultimately, these are very Pan-African hairstyles." While the renowned hairstylist laments the fact that many women in Africa continue to alter their hair under the weight of sometimes toxic beauty dictates—poisonous thinking inherited from colonization and slavery, and sometimes perpetuated by African hairstylists themselves, who stigmatize natural hair—in the last few years, she has observed a new enthusiasm for these vibrant signature looks. "Some people see it as a political approach; to me it's a way of leading my personal revolution. Hairstyle is my heritage."

Founded in the late 1990s, Afropunk—a legendary event where alternative Black cultures and music come together—has become the preferred setting for celebrating African aesthetics. Colorful braids or locs, blue lips inspired by Peul tattoos and makeup by the tribes of the Omo Valley in Ethiopia, *isicholo* headdresses,[16] *xibelani* dance skirts,[17] East African *kikoys*,[18] and wax-print designs: a proud, socially engaged generation employs

Trevor Stuurman and Manthe Ribane modeling looks inspired by the film *Black Panther* that they created at the request of the Marvel and Disney studios, February 2018.
© Obakeng Molepe.

147. Style

Malian women wearing boubous, 2002.
© Catherine Laurent.

TREND

TRADITION

Blouses, dress, and *batakali* tunics by Marché Noir (brand created by Amah Ayivi), June 2019. © Marc Posso.

REND

and revisits the symbols of an abundantly diverse African continent. The body becomes a means to create unity. "Because our experience in white-dominated nation-states inflicts perpetual violence against our sense of self, Afropunk has become an oasis of Blackness that allows the flowers of our consciousness to grow freely," explains Anita Asante, Global Strategic Brand Partnerships Lead for Afropunk Worldwide. "We have always been aesthetic geniuses. Throughout the diaspora, Black people use fashion as a medium to express their emotions. Fashion by its nature is of the body, and the Black body has been made an inherently political space. At Afropunk festivals, some of the fashion interrogates ideas of gender, sexuality, humanity, violence, and tribal identity—and it's beautiful to behold."

Designers, stylists, musicians, dancers, and bloggers from across the continent are also exploring these ideas. Many of them are working, above all, to deconstruct stereotypes and, through their innovative style, invent a new way of being African today, independent of uniforms, obsolete images, and fantasies. By elevating boldness and cross-cultural hybridity to a new "way of life," they are influencing their entire generation. Tilila Oulhaj, muse of Maison ART/C and Mous Lamrabat, makes intentionally "political" choices when selecting her collaborators (as she explains on p. 190). In the images composed by these two Moroccan artists, Oulhaj is never depicted as the odalisque expected by the Western gaze, but as a woman of the Global South who embodies, one after another, the myriad faces of her native Morocco without falling into cliché. She refuses to let her face, with skin suggestive of a henna design, become a label, and she criticizes the Orientalist fetishization to which she is at times subjected.

Combining humor and poetry, finesse and tenderness, South African Nikiwe Dlova (see p. 191) draws inspiration from the art of African headdresses to create her lyrical hair sculptures. Because nothing is more vulnerable than when it is static, she imbues these sculptures with her penchant for playfulness, joyful experimentation, and a hint of the future. As does her fellow countrywoman and singer Pilani Bubu (see pp. 166–67), whose healer spirit as well as aesthetics infuse her music: "I like people

to be able to realize the potential of their imaginations. And how imagination comes from nothing. Turning what is personal to me into something that resonates with others and inspires them is what allows us, artists, to free others by freeing ourselves." This freedom is also expressed in the personal style of Cameroonian photographer Louis Philippe de Gagoue, who, for years before his untimely death in August 2021, took his unrestrained looks into the streets of Paris, Casablanca, Abidjan, Milan, and beyond. The undisputed master of reappropriation and culture clash, he was an alchemist who saw beauty everywhere and dared to try anything. Sporting psychedelic blue leggings, a skirt in recycled plastic, an Indian headdress, or a basketweave plastron by Selly Raby Kane, this fascinating sartorial dabbler and dazzling stylist challenged, questioned, and expanded the range of possibilities for all men.

In a similar vein, Ivorian designer Loza Maléombho creates a female character of such singularity that she becomes an archetype—a new model that broadens the spectrum of feminine representation. She wears her own designs, a repertory of African inspirations in which hessian meets bronze, and raffia engages with plastic, composing looks that are as sexy as they are avant garde. With her bold look, she is the epitome of the emancipated, multifaceted woman steeped in several cultures by her personal history and travels. Much the same can be said for Senegalese designer Selly Raby Kane, whose sartorial offerings with a futuristic flair also reinvent the codes of femininity. South African photographer and artistic director Trevor Stuurman is also, in his own way, a multifaceted character. A style icon in Africa and an ultra-modern, globetrotting dandy, Stuurman delights street-style photographers from Johannesburg to Milan. A fan of captivating mix-and-match looks who effortlessly pairs a Senegalese boubou with a white Stetson hat, *izimbadada* sandals[19] with an Afrofuturist T-shirt, or a wax-print suit with white Doc Martens embellished with a red heart, Stuurman deconstructs outdated clichés of African men. He is also a committed supporter of African

Facing page:
Kenyan artist Velma
Rossa, 2017.
© Sarah Waiswa.

Left:
Clint Malik,
March 2018.
© Rogers Ouma (M. Ojwook).

"There's something Afrofuturist about this photo: the *ndokette* dress, with its voluminous sleeves that resemble a spacesuit's; the flashy color of my boubou; the white glasses; the umbrella; Trevor's babouches. Some people see me as 'the girl with the scarf and weird accessories,' or the daughter of a marabout, because I wear loose clothing. But my boubou collection 'Sidi' was inspired by my grandfather's wardrobe. I took some of his clothes and wore one of his boubous to a wedding, but since I don't know how to walk in heels, I wore sneakers. Even before I created L'Artisane, people wanted to wear what I was wearing, because what I wear tells a story."

Khadija Aisha Ba
FOUNDER OF L'ARTISANE
@lartisane.shop

Trevor Stuurman,
Khadija Aisha Ba,
and Mamy Tall wearing
boubous by L'Artisane
(brand created by
Khadija Aisha Ba),
from the "Sidi"
collection, Dakar,
2018.
©Tsholofelo Kodisang.

Dan men from Ivory Coast wearing boubous and
tarbouche caps, Man region, Ivory Coast, 1971.

Khadija Aisha Ba, founder of L'Artisane, wearing her "Khari" boubou, Dakar, 2018.

TREND

brands—including Laurence Airline, Thebe Magugu, Studio One Eighty Nine, and Simon and Mary. Like many of his peers, Stuurman often collaborates with other talented individuals (in his case, with artist Manthe Ribane and the @dearribane113 collective) to write what they call "a new African narrative."

Certain artists, like Belgian-Congolese musician and visual artist Baloji or Petite Noir in their videos or films, demonstrate an aesthetic that, along with the music they compose, urges viewers to fully accept themselves as cosmopolitan. Each artist in their own way, and for various reasons, gives form to Alioune Sall's conviction that clinging to a single idea of African identity or being engulfed by globalization are two sure ways to lose oneself.[20] Both musicians invite a revolutionary shift in perspective through their dreamlike tales. A brilliant, extraordinary poet, Baloji denounces in his music video "Zombies" and short film *Kaniama Show*[21] the "sleeping sickness" that subjugates African people. In all his videos, which he constructs like paintings, there is something "creole"—pool sliders and a revisited ritual mask, a tailored suit and a marriage altar made of corn cobs and banana leaves. In his world, the streets of Kinshasa are populated with many different creatures, from fragile waifs to unfettered women, or from *sapeurs* in pink suits to vogueurs[22] in yellow tutus. Baloji unsettles the imagination and tears down real, normative, and psychological walls—as does Yannick Ilunga, alias Petite Noir, creator of Noirwave,[23] a movement that aspires to be the reflection and echo of the "interior landscape" of all those who are originally from Africa, or have lived there, and who find themselves stuck "in between" cultures. His aesthetic straddles tribute, citation, and Afrofuturist dream, and unsettles secular signposts and labels. The body is the place where eras are defined, and the space where freedom is won.

"Instagram plays an important role in the changes taking place in the African fashion scene. Designers record their stories, their environment, their travels, and their discoveries. Every image they publish is a little piece of Africa that says something about our cultures and our experiences. Thanks to this, influences have shifted, and the Global South now takes more of its influence from the Global South itself."

Emmanuel Ekuban
FOUNDER OF THE PLATFORM AND INSTAGRAM ACCOUNT @DEBONAIR

Architect Mamy Tall
wearing an ensemble
by L'Artisane
(brand created by
Khadija Aisha Ba),
from the 2020
collection, Dakar.
©Déthié Diagne – @thefreeminds.
Courtesy Mamy Tall.

"I would describe my style as vintage West Africa meets modernist diaspora. Family portraits and the works of Ojeikere, as well as Nollywood films and hip-hop music videos from the 1990s and early 2000s, are constant inspirations for my hair and style decisions. I particularly enjoy recreating old African hairstyles from the 1960s and 1970s. This hairstyle was inspired by Ojeikere's iconic images. I opted for orange thread, which adds a pop of color. I remember watching my mother get dressed for Nigerian parties and being so enamored with her style. She would tie her *gele* and step out with the most intricately woven *aso-oke* fabrics paired with 'roach killers'—pointed-toe, kitten-heel shoes. She always had a way of making something traditional appear slightly alternative. I credit her with inspiring my taste for bold pairings."

Erykah Ijeoma Achebe
STYLIST AND MANAGER OF A CREATIVE AGENCY IN NEW YORK
@erykahachebe @achebevennfrederic

Erykah Ijeoma Achebe,
self-portrait, 2020.
Hair: Wow African Hair
Braiding.
© Erykah Ijeoma Achebe.

TRADITION

Rwandan man with a traditional Amasunzu hairstyle, by Casimir Zagourski, postcard, *Rwanda: A Mutudzi*, no. 89, series 1: "L'Afrique qui disparaît!," 1929–37, 5½ × 3½ in. (14 × 9 cm). The Eliot Elisofon Photographic Archives, National Museum of African

TREND

"I became obsessed with beading as a craft and with the way that various sizes and styles of beads can have a cultural and spiritual significance. I move from the signature black beads to wooden ones to beads in a variety of colors based on the mood and style cues I would like to bring into my look. The theme is driven by whatever music project I am working on at the time. Naturally, I have always been bold in my expression, and visual cues mean something to me. My intention is always to tell a story that will shift people's perspective or create a place of resonance. I want to inspire people to embrace their heritage and all that comes with it."

Pilani Bubu
ARTIST, CULTURAL ENTREPRENEUR, AND TELEVISION PRESENTER
@pilanibubu

Members of the group
V.I.N.T.A.G.E Crew,
South Africa.
© Daniele Tamagni.
Courtesy Giordano Tamagni.

Heavy metal enthusiast,
Gaborone, Botswana.
© Daniele Tamagni.
Courtesy Giordano Tamagni.

Congolese *sapeur* in
front of Cléo's hair
salon in the Bacongo
district, Brazzaville,
Republic of Congo.
© Baudouin Mouanda.

Facing page:
Chadi, Casablanca,
Morocco, 2018.
© Joseph Ouechen.

Below:
Artist Kabeya Mikishi Mokeli wearing a mask sculpted by Junior Mvunzi Muteba of the Bakeli collective, in *Sinnerman, a Portrait of _* by Prisca Munkeni Monnier, Kinshasa, Kintambo, Democratic Republic of Congo, from the "La Vie Est Belle" series produced for *Off To* magazine, Kinshasa issue, 2020.
© Prisca Munkeni Monnier.

Facing page:
Artist Kabeya Mikishi Mokeli wearing a pair of wings in steel sculpted by Junior Mvunzi Muteba of the Bakeli collective, in *Mabele Y'a Mboka* by Prisca Munkeni Monnier, Kinshasa, Democratic Republic of Congo, from the "La Vie Est Belle" series, published on the cover of *Off To* magazine, Kinshasa issue, 2020.
© Prisca Munkeni Monnier.

Page 178:
Selly Raby Kane.
© Jean-Baptiste Joire.

Page 179:
Manthe Ribane
and Trevor Stuurman
wearing hats created
by Trevor Stuurman.
© Simz Photo.

Above:
Congolese artist Baloji
wearing an outfit he
created himself and a
mask by Damselfrau
(Magnhild Kennedy),
still from Baloji's
short film *Peau de
Chagrin/Bleu de Nuit*,
March 2018.
© Kristin Lee Moolman.

Facing page:
Loza Maléombho
modeling a look from
her spring–summer
2019 collection.
© Cee Aloukou.
Courtesy Loza Maléombho.

Musician Ibaaku
(Stephen Ibaaku
Bassene) in a building
under construction in
Dakar, Senegal,
advertising campaign
for his first album,
Alien Cartoon,
released in 2016.

"I built my style the way I would build a palace. I want every single piece to be artistic and perfect, starting from my hats and the contrast with my black skin, the details on my clothes and shoes. The people who I came across in the streets and who became models for my projects are like me; they want to tell a story that they can't talk about for some reason. I don't use Photoshop, I work with daylight; everything is natural. I want to show the reality in my photos and the diversity in our society. Instagram is one of the—if not the— best platforms to get noticed. That's how the gallery that represents my work found me."

Abdel Queta Tavares
ARTIST
@abdelkeitatavares

Abdel Queta Tavares,
self-portrait, from
the "Sapeur" series,
2018.
© Abdel Queta Tavares.

Trevor Stuurman

VISUAL ARTIST @trevor_stuurman

"Africans in the past were not photographed by Africans, but by others. Now, we have the power to change that. I have done a lot of work with the continent's fashion designers: with South Africans Rich Mnisi and Laduma for Maxhosa, with Laurence Airline from Ivory Coast, and Ushie from Ghana. These are the fashion designers who have inspired me the most, and together we are building a new visual language, which future generations will be able to refer to. Our images, the ones I make, and the clothes created by these designers, will allow them to say 'this is what Africa looks like.' It is not only about changing the narrative, but also about reclaiming dignity, restoring pride, and empowering Africa. Thus, for example, while 'Made in Africa' was traditionally considered 'cheap,' now it has acquired new value. Thanks to *ELLE South Africa*—for which I documented South African culture, followed the continent's fashion weeks, and traveled around the world—I learned the power of storytelling. It made me more conscious and aware of my responsibilities as a publisher and of how we can use information to empower ourselves and others.

The people I photograph look like some kind of ideal. Some even look like superheroes: they make me dream bigger. When I photographed myself in Dakar, with a large embroidered boubou made by Senegalese brand L'Artisane, it made me feel royal, it made me feel powerful. This is the power of clothes, and it goes a long way, because this kind of fashion image might inspire someone else who will also want to radiate his own power. Now that things have changed, especially in terms of the production of images, the power of influence is with us."

Trevor Stuurman,
self-portrait wearing
a boubou by L'Artisane
(brand created by
Khadija Aisha Ba),
2019.
© Trevor Stuurman.

Nontsikelelo Veleko

PHOTOGRAPHER @nontsikelelovlk

> I got the idea for 'Beauty Is in the Eye of the Beholder,' my initial series about street style, in 2003 in Switzerland, during my first photography residency. My friends were shopping every weekend, buying 'fast fashion,' and I was disgusted by the waste, but also by the lack of imagination on their part. I thought back to the styles I saw worn by certain students in Cape Town; how they stood out from the crowd with clothes they had made themselves, but also how they had to endure mean stares, ridicule, and sometimes even physical violence.
>
> It was a time of great change in South African life and politics, but also in photography. Up to that point, photography had mainly focused on documenting apartheid. In South Africa, and Africa as a whole, we were bombarded with negative images of ourselves. Mandela's freedom was experienced as a collective freedom, and we all took part in it by expressing our hopes and aspirations. When I spoke to these young people, I found out they were actually their own 'walking billboards' for their creations and that blew my mind. They expressed the freedom to decide their fate. This is what fashion was to me: a statement, a form of evoking emotions, and I found that beautiful and daring.
>
> 'Street style' definitely plays a special role in influencing fashion. It could even be a starting point for a designer to understand the spirit of the times. I remember *Vogue* mentioning a look I photographed in 2003 that made its international runway debut years later, in 2012. At the time they were asking questions like, 'So who influences whom? Is it Africa that influences Europe or vice versa?'

Nontsikelelo Veleko
in 2021.
© Georges Courrèges.

Karim Chater in 2021.
© Adil Daaji.

Karim Chater

STREET ARTIST @style_beldi

" Through my Instagram videos and posts, I showcase Moroccan culture and lifestyle to the rest of the world. I get my inspiration from my childhood, my parents' lifestyle, our Moroccan traditions, and my neighborhood in Casablanca: Sidi Moumen, near the shantytown of Rhamna. When I discovered the style my parents had in the 1970s, I immediately fell in love with vintage fashion and became a big fan of how people dressed back then.

I was inspired to bring back that incredible style while adding my own personal touch.

I shop mostly at Moroccan thrift shops. Vintage style is rarely represented here in Morocco, and most people just go with the flow and adopt the latest trends. It is my duty to keep reminding people how amazing, unique, and very high quality vintage clothing can be. My style changes from time to time, depending on what I want people to understand from a picture or video.

The important thing for me is to present the different cultures within my country, and that requires showcasing different styles to illustrate each one fairly. Africa is a rich continent with thousands of different cultures, and we must keep them alive by creating and drawing inspiration from each one.

Style Beldi is not just an Instagram account; for me, it is a source of pride and motivation to continue what I started, keeping in mind the simple circumstances in which I began. One of my biggest goals is to display my environment as it is, in all its realism, to the rest of the world. To me, beauty is showing things without a filter. I try my best to make my Moroccan audience proud of every piece of content I put out there. The Internet is a small place with billions of users, and I always make sure that my art deserves to be seen. Social networks have definitely made it easy for youngsters to present themselves and their art, and to tell their stories. It's less intimidating now than it must have been thirty years ago. "

Tilila Oulhaj

MODEL @808tilly

" Some people see my freckles as a 'singularity' representative of a presumed identity. But the human relationship to identity is many-layered, and, while they are a part of me, I don't glorify them or consider them a defining characteristic of my identity. There is a difference in how I am looked at in my country, Morocco, and abroad, where I am 'othered' and subjected to clichés and stereotypes.

Regardless of empty attempts at 'multiculturalism' and 'inclusion,' Western beauty standards are still the default. When I'm not being subjugated through blatant racism, fetishism, sexualization, and Orientalist fantasies, I am subjected to more casual approaches, like glorification, being put on a pedestal, or over-complementing.

The body will be truly decolonized when Moroccan women are no longer represented in history and the media as sexualized, limited, restricted, or devalued—when the tall, skinny, blonde, blue-eyed woman ceases to be the epitome of beauty. Of course, there are spaces where my identity as a Brown woman [living in the Global South] is neither over-hyped nor reduced, but there are fundamental things that have to change: not just representation, but also the material conditions of beauty standards, so that we no longer even have to use words like 'inclusion.'

I collaborate primarily with Moroccans, and Maison ART/C in particular. The message is simple: celebrate Moroccan culture, Moroccan imagination, and Moroccan creativity in an independent space where you don't have to reference it back to a Western or 'white-washed' view, where it can exist for its own sake, in its own greatness, completely detached from comparisons. Plainly and simply reclaiming our culture and representing it ourselves, for us and for the world. "

Tilila Oulhaj modeling a look by Maison ART/C.

Courtesy Maison ART/C.

Nikiwe Dlova

ARTIST
FOUNDER OF @OWNURCROWN
@nix_indamix

> Until recently, people were not really open to creative African hairstyles because, for so long, they weren't seen enough. People had moved away from these creative styles due to colonization and the trend for straight hair. Institutions also had a huge role to play in this because, between school—where there were rules about how your hair should be—and work, where only slick, straight hair was seen as 'professional'—South Africans didn't really have room to explore hairstyles. 'Own Ur Crown' is about celebrating our royal blood. I want everyone to celebrate who they are, and also to inspire people not to be scared to be themselves, to be creative and bold.

Before it was an Instagram account, Own Ur Crown started as a blog with the same aim: I wanted people to see hair as part of their identity and lifestyle. I interviewed artists and hairstylists. I felt like people weren't celebrating those hairstyles enough, and to inspire them, I merged pre-colonial traditional hairstyles with a modern look, which is why I prefer to call these new hairstyles 'creative,' rather than traditional. The first style I created in 2016 was inspired by Yoruba women in Nigeria and a threading style we normally do in South Africa. Some people made fun of it, others liked it; but the whole point was to get people used to seeing crazy, cool African hairstyles.

When people started asking me where I got my hair done, I saw there was a need and started a platform that provides hairstyling services. I also create headpieces, like the one I made for Beyoncé, inspired by Zulu *isicholo* headpieces fused with other elements of South African cultures. Being African is my main source of inspiration. We must remember that we are descended from royal ancestors. I see hairstyles as a form of political expression. "

n just two decades, Malian photographers Malick Sidibé and Seydou Keïta have come to be regarded as icons of African photography, by both the art world and a mainstream international audience. Like other West African portrait photographers working in the years between 1950 and 1980, they captured snapshots of daily life, of families, and of individual mannerisms. But in doing so, and through their unique attention to dress, these photographers unintentionally created a record of trends and notions of elegance. From a contemporary Western perspective, fashion photography is associated with glossy magazines, with advertising and selling clothes, but the reality is far more complex in Africa. The fashion and ready-to-wear industry, as well as the press outlets that publish this kind of photography, have only recently emerged on the continent. For many years, the legendary *Revue Noire*[1] was the only publication to accept work by African fashion photographers and to commission images for specific issues. The excitement surrounding this body of work and the interest it generated in the late 2010s was a result of three converging phenomena: the dawn of Tumblr, blogs, and Instagram; the emergence of branding; and the development of specialized reviews and magazines. For many young African artists, the Internet and related digital tools have provided a springboard for presenting their work, and have given street-style photographers, designers, and many "image makers" a way to introduce the world to a new aesthetic. Indeed, this is how South African visual artist Trevor Stuurman and Ivorian-Cameroonian stylist and photographer Louis Philippe de Gagoue were discovered: through their visionary self-representations (see Style chapter), which, as they were welcomed into new circles, enabled them to expand on their talents. But Instagram poses certain risks for fashion photographers—when their work is endlessly reposted by "curator" accounts, inspiring thousands of followers, it can lead to excessive imitation. How many budding photographers, after witnessing the meteoric rise of artist Kvvadwo,[2] have created strikingly similar images, in which the blackness of the subject's skin—edited to remove distinctive

Facing page:
Photograph by Louis Philippe de Gagoue for the editorial "Ghetto Symphony," *Now Fashion* magazine, 2016, featuring Kady Coulibaly modeling clothing from Ground Zero's spring–summer 2016 collection.
© Louis Philippe de Gagoue.

Page 196:
Photograph by Louis Philippe de Gagoue, *Chouf Chouf*, Ivory Coast.
© Louis Philippe de Gagoue.

Page 197:
Photograph by Louis Philippe de Gagoue, *La Panthère Noire* (The Black Panther), Ivory Coast.
© Louis Philippe de Gagoue.

facial features—contrasts with deep, vibrant colors? "Instagram is wonderful for creating an audience and getting noticed," says Marie Gomis-Trezise, founder of the agency Galerie Number 8[3] and creative director of Nataal Media,[4] which describes itself as a global media brand celebrating contemporary African fashion, music, arts and society. "But it can also contribute to depreciating artists' work by taking each image out of context, out of the series to which it belongs, and separating it from a particular message." In the 2010s, Nataal Media marked a turning point by launching an annual showcase for African fashion photography, both online and in print. *Vogue Italia* did much the same, giving many African artists the opportunity to publish their images or articles on its website; in this way, the magazine called attention to the younger generation of Africa's fashion scene. As new brands emerge, along with the many online stores that distribute them, there is an attendant need to publicize these creations—and fashion photography is exploding in response. "Many of these artists work collaboratively," explains Gomis-Trezise. "They are a bold generation. They didn't wait to be recognized as artistic directors by someone externally or someone older." Some of them take on different roles from one series to the next, assuming the mantle of photographer, stylist, artistic director, or artist. Some have even launched their own publications, such as *Faculty Press*, a "bible" of South African fashion created by Thebe Magugu in 2019, and *Nikkou*, the first multicultural magazine to bring together fashion, luxury, and contemporary art, created by Louis Philippe de Gagoue the same year. Unlike in other publications, Africa appears not as a backdrop, but rather as a narrative with a pioneering approach to aesthetics. The reviews *Oath*[5] and *SWAG*[6] also commission and publish fashion photography. "Magazines are powerful, physical, tangible entities that contribute to celebrating a culture or shaping a movement, and there is so much to celebrate in South Africa and beyond," says Stephanie Blomkamp, founder and editor of *Oath* magazine. "There is an abundance of photographic talent in Africa that deserves a great platform." While photographers like Lakin Ogunbanwo, Daniel Obasi, and Nadine Ijewere, among others,

Below:
Photograph by Louis Philippe de Gagoue, *Mami N'yanga*, for the brand EDUN, featuring Emmanuella Kamenan modeling clothing from the fall-winter 2016 collection, Yamassoukro, Ivory Coast, 2016.
© Louis Philippe de Gagoue.

Facing page:
Photograph by Louis Philippe de Gagoue, *Azambo Wama*, for the brand EDUN, featuring Emmanuella Kamenan modeling clothing from the fall-winter 2016 collection, Yamassoukro, Ivory Coast, 2016.
© Louis Philippe de Gagoue.

have participated in publicity campaigns to promote African brands, and others still have received commissions from leading international fashion publications, many also—and above all—describe themselves as "image makers," for whom clothing serves as a tool for spreading a message. "It is used to tell stories that are not relative to the product itself," remarks Blomkamp. "I believe that photography across Africa is part of a much greater phenomenon: it is an affirmation of identity, a celebration of culture, a possession of self." With their evocative power, fashion images form part of this movement, since, as Nigerian photographer Stephen Tayo explains, "What people wear or how they dress has so much to do with where they are from and where they live."

Fashion photography has always held up a mirror to society, one that allows us to self-project and to construct our identity, as well as to represent the Other. It also enables new standards of beauty, capable of transforming society, to emerge. African photography introduces a new aesthetic entirely unlike conventional binary representations—distinctly "Western" features versus objects of fantasy far removed from the established canons of beauty in their own countries—that reflect a single way of thinking about the African continent and are incapable of capturing the diversity of Black expressions of beauty. Black skin and the white skin of people living with albinism become subjects in their own right. Exalted through strong contrasts that only enhance their beauty, painted in yellow like Gouro ritual masks, as in the work of artist Nuits Balnéaires, or in metallic blue by Manthe Ribane or Mous Lamrabat, dressed up in tights or adorned with body paint, they reflect the light that illuminates them anew. Emancipated locks come into their own, in innovative hairstyles or adorned with accessories. Mouths are accentuated with blue outlines and male eyelids shimmer with colorful shadow. Colors are incandescent, humor scathing, and all inhibition abandoned. The work of Rafael Pavarotti, Ibrahim Kamara, Louis Philippe de Gagoue, and Daniel Obasi shatters social conventions in order to reinvent them. Praising culture, gender fluidity, and interculturality, each photographer broadens the field of possible representations. Through its power to

change the way we view the world and the cultures of Africa and its diasporas, fashion photography becomes a political act, and clothing is the vocabulary used to express it. Androgynous bodies and sexual ambiguity expressed through gender-neutral clothing choices challenge social strictures. This focus is present in many of the series by Anglo-Nigerian photographer Ruth Ossai, including "Homecoming," which depicts emerging African fashion brands distributed by the English luxury boutique Browns (see p. 205). World-renowned photographer Hassan Hajjaj, known for his works that celebrate popular Moroccan and other African cultures, deconstructs the way Arab women are viewed—often as objects of persistent stereotypes rooted in the history of colonization. Playing with these clichés, he reproduces poses, which have long been popular in European painting, depicting women as lascivious odalisques, and he injects them with a dose of pop culture that has become his signature; his use of humor forces viewers to question the power of their gaze—and how it shapes their thinking. This is evident in the series "Kesh Angels" (a play on the name of the famous motorcycle gang), in which women bikers dressed in polka-dot djellabas, customized babouches, heart-shaped glasses, and scarves or veils covering their hair and faces, challenge preconceived ideas. Moroccan photographer Mous Lamrabat also plays with brand logos, combining them with elements from African culture: in one image, a figure wears a bead-encrusted Bamileke elephant mask, to which the artist has added the Nike logo—a "swoosh" of cowrie shells that speaks to his own diverse cultural heritage. He loves "combining things that don't belong together," as he puts it, "because my greatest source of inspiration lies in my many identities. I always see myself in relation to what I am and what I feel as a Moroccan, an African, and a Muslim." This taste for cultural collage, for a mash-up of references, is shared by many African artists who have been nomads since childhood and have felt the gaze of others questioning their identities.

Reappropriating one's image is a way of presenting a personal perception of one's environment; or it is at least an attempt to illustrate that environment without artifice, transforming what others

Top:
Nikkou (no. 1, summer 2019), biannual magazine created by Louis Philippe de Gagoue.
Cover (featuring Naomi Campbell) and double-page spread.
© Louis Philippe de Gagoue.

Center:
Faculty Press (no. 1, "African Studies," 2019), annual magazine created by Thebe Magugu.
Cover: styling by Thebe Magugu.
© Travys Owen.
Double-page spread: photographs by Jacques Wayers. Clothing: Nao Serati. Hair and makeup: Orli Meiri.
© Jacques Weyers.

Bottom: *Nataal* (no. 2, June 2019).
Cover: photograph by Mous Lamrabat. Models: Jean Severin and Patrick Kouadio. Styling: Lisa Lapauw.
© Mous Lamrabat.
Double-page spread: "Love Buzz," photographs by Nadine Ijewere. Models: Magueye Diouck and Anna Sophie (Akray Agency), Helena Mahama (Premier). Styling: Nathan Klein. Hair: Cyndia Harvey.
© Nadine Ijewere.

Page 202:
Photograph by Nadine Ijewere, from the "Portraits of Young People in Lagos" series, Lagos, Nigeria, 2017. Styling: Ibrahim Kamara.
© Nadine Ijewere/Trunk Archive/PhotoSenso.

Page 203:
Photograph by Nuits Balnéaires, for Yhebe Design (brand created by Rebecca Zoro), from the "Lou" collection. Models: Fatima Kouamé and Leila Evelyne. Makeup: Kiela Annie.
© Nuits Balnéaires.

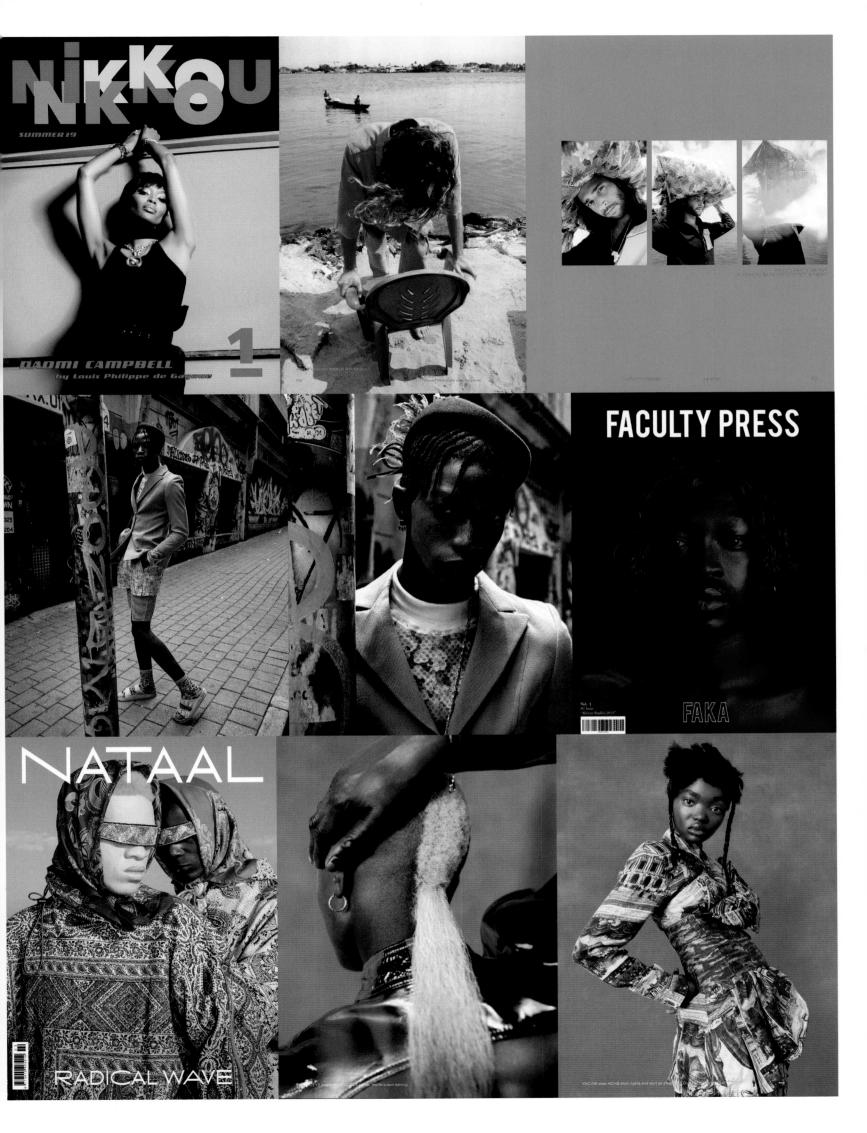

"Fashion photography, which focuses on portraiture, posing, extensive lighting, beautiful locations, and clothing, is evolving rapidly, as many photographers find new channels for and ways to create their own aesthetic. By creating new narratives, they are transforming perceptions of fashion."

Richmond Orlando Mensah
CREATIVE DIRECTOR AND FOUNDER OF MANJU JOURNAL
@manjujournal

Photograph by
Jonathan Kope for *ELLE
South Africa*, Soweto,
Johannesburg, South
Africa, May 2018.
Model: Sayra Jatto.
Styling: Asanda
Sizani. Hair: Emelang
Moyo. Makeup:
Caroline Greef.
© Jonathan Kope.

see as refuse into the shining material of composition. Depicting a clash of cultures is a familiar concept in fashion photography, and Louis Philippe de Gagoue was one African photographer to have mastered it. Unlike images shaped by the Western gaze, featuring white models draped in haute couture dresses and depicting members of local communities as "extras" who are entirely unaware of the issues at stake in the images in which they appear, the work of De Gagoue represents modern Africans at the heart of a fearless and filterless Africa: red laterite roads in the Cameroonian bush; brutalist architecture in Yaoundé and Abidjan; the beaches of Grand-Bassam; and the historic, working-class neighborhood of Jamestown in Accra, Ghana. Debris-strewn spaces, coal-blackened mud-brick walls, chaotic traffic: while a "culture of ugliness" is all the rage in the West, De Gagoue saw only beauty in its representations. For this photographer, who loved combining luxury and underground culture with the decadence of certain African environments, even the polluted banks of the Ebrié Lagoon in Ivory Coast were a worthy backdrop for the creatures he clothed in his own imaginative style. He condemned nothing; rather, he offered a new way of seeing the world.

Similarly, in addition to her vibrant work for the world's leading international fashion magazines, including *Vogue* and *Dazed*, British photographer Nadine Ijewere, of Nigerian and Jamaican heritage, explores the singular character of the young people living in her grandmother's home town in the series "Portraits of Young People in Lagos." In the photos, everyday accessories including colorful colanders, boxing gloves, a bridal veil, plastic bags, and a green bucket, unearthed at local markets by star designer of Sierra Leone origin Ibrahim Kamara, are turned into inventive looks and jewelry that reflect a spirited patchwork of identities embedded in the urban environment—an iconoclastic approach that challenges the eye. In Mous Lamrabat's work, a woman holding a chicken outside an earthen house is transformed into a work of classical art. Like many artists of his generation, he is a "third culture kid"[7]: "Our roots are intensely alive," says Lamrabat. Each summer, he traveled to his parents' village in Morocco,

Below:
Photograph by Hassan Hajjaj, *S.P. Bikin'*, 2015. The wood frame is inlaid with cans of Aicha tomatoes.
© Hassan Hajjaj.
Courtesy of the artist.

Facing page:
Photograph by Artsimous (Artsi Ifrach and Mous Lamrabat) featuring Tilila Oulhaj, from the "Village" series, 2019. Clothing: Maison ART/C.
© Artsimous (Artsi Ifrach and Mous Lamrabat).

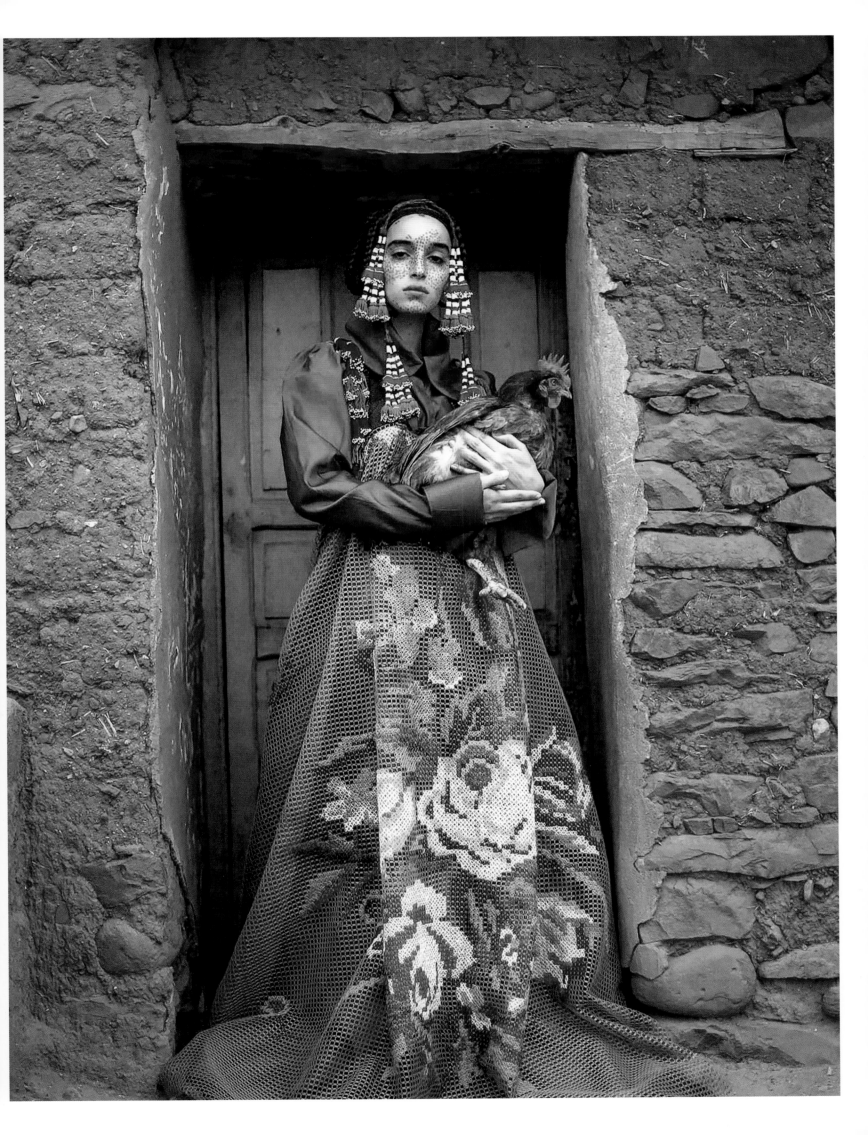

where he photographed glasses, plates, rounds of Laughing Cow cheese at the corner store, and the motley assortment of objects that he discovered in souks. He found inspiration in everything—and still does today. "I realized that people no longer found beauty in these things," he observes. Because all migrants and immigrants question their identity(ies), the contrasts that infuse his work serve to "valorize that which we are no longer able to view as beautiful in our environment and our cultures." According to the photographer, "fashion photography is a way of thinking."

This process of revealing beauty can also be seen in the series "Strong Women" by Rwandan artist Cedric Mizero. A collaboration with photographer Chris Schwagga, the series celebrates the energy and strength of women from Mizero's home village, Gishoma. Because he "enjoys exploring the possibilities of fabric, and because clothes are elements that attract the public's attention," he asked the women to wear dresses and accessories, quite unlike their usual attire, that he had made himself. In this way, Mizero destroys the boundaries of our representations: through the power of fashion, these everyday heroines emerge as strong women with a voice and presence. "The environment that photographers or visual artists live in or have lived in is an essential part of themselves, so including it in honest detail is part of telling a story, and of being true to oneself," says Stephanie Blomkamp.

By his own admission, Ivorian visual artist Kader Diaby belongs to "a generation that accepts what it is and where it comes from," and photographing "the organized disorder and chaos of cities serves as an aesthetic and a message." He chose the entrance halls and roofs of dilapidated buildings in Abidjan's business district, Le Plateau, as the backdrop for his series "Feuillet" in order to position his message within the environment of the people it is intended to reach—and, consequently, to raise awareness among his fellow citizens about the ravages of fast fashion. He dresses his models in paper garments that contribute to a critique of throwaway fashion and implicitly denounce secondhand clothing, which destroys local textile industries. Ghanaian artist Sackitey Tesa also explores this phenomenon in his photographic work. The son of a costume designer, he learned at an early age to assemble fabrics and materials and, like many Ghanaians, to recycle *obroni wawu*. Literally meaning "dead white men's clothes," the name is derived from the belief that imported textile waste results from the death of the garments' former owners. "The power of art lies in its ability to start a conversation, and this work seeks to do that," he says of his photograph *Yesterday's Shopping* (see p. 210). In it, two masculine figures bound in plastic corsets, standing in front of huge sacks of plastic bottles, address the essential need for recycling and the role that the fashion industry—and fashion photography—can play in this century's greatest struggle.

Fashion photography cultivates a close connection with time. References to previous artistic currents are common. Many members of this young generation, for example, pay tribute to the studio tradition: in his series "Studio of the Vanities," Omar Victor Diop captured Dakar's youthful, creative generation in all its finery. Fabrics and emerging fashion labels (like Selly Raby Kane and her blue cardigans, see p. 217) bear witness to a changing era, stamped with the seal of filiation. In other cases, it is through references to the tradition of plein air photography—such as in the fashion mise-en-scènes photographed in the street by Stephen Tayo—that the most significant African brands, including Orange Culture and Post-Imperial, reveal their powerful modernity, strengthened by their adherence to past conventions. Ruth Ossai also pays homage to African visual traditions in her work, taking inspiration (as in her "Homecoming" series: see p. 205) from the aesthetics in Nollywood movies and in music videos of Igbo traditional music from Nigeria. Fashion photography is a reflection of society—of its taboos, its desires, and its anxieties—and an image of the present, but at times it is also a laboratory where the future is conceived or imagined. In his series "Lagos Futurism," visual artist William Ukoh,[8] of Nigerian heritage, uses clothing as the vocabulary for an Afrofuturist line of thought, one inspired by classism in Nigeria. "This was the inspiration for the characters I chose to create. With the styling, I wanted something dynamic and visually arresting." In one image, a slender figure

Photograph by Cedric Mizero from the "Strong Women" series, in collaboration with Chris Schwagga.
© Cedric Mizero.

213.

overlooks the city, inspired by designer Loza Maléombho's series "Alien Edits" (see pp. 228–29) and wearing one of her creations. The image speaks to the society evoked by the artist in her selfie series, in which Black women would be able to move through the world, tall and proud, unhindered by worldly concerns like racism and condescension. Ukoh combines designer brands (I.AM.ISIGO and Orange Culture) with Nigerian embroidery, *gele* headscarves, and aluminum foil. In collaboration with designer Daniel Obasi, he composes a painterly, radiant, and dreamlike portrait of an alternative city, post protestations. For therein lies the power of fashion photography, clothing, and jewelry: to provide a vocabulary of emancipation and freedom. As Marie Gomis-Trezise quite rightly reminds us, "African photographers don't only photograph Black people or African stories in Africa." As has been shown in previous chapters, each of the best of them makes a unique contribution to revolutionizing the way we perceive the world, the way the West views Africa and Africans, and the way Africans see their environment and their history. With these creators, it is no longer just a question of fostering a diversity of cultures and viewpoints, but also of inventing the worlds of tomorrow.

Below and facing page: Photographs by Kader Diaby from the "Feuillet" series, Abidjan, Ivory Coast, for the webzine *BTendance*, 2017. Styling: Kader Diaby and Rebecca Zoro. Makeup: Fatou Diaby.

Page 216: Photograph by Namsa Leuba, *Untitled III*, from the "Cocktail" series, published in *WAD Magazine* (no. 53, summer 2012).

Page 217: Photograph by Omar Victor Diop, *Alt + Shift + Ego*, featuring singer Adama Boudoir modeling two cardigans created by Selly Raby Kane, 2013.

Above, left:
Photograph by
Seydou Keïta,
Untitled, Bamako,
Mali, 1948–54.
© Seydou Keïta / SKPEAC.
Courtesy The Jean Pigozzi
Collection of African Art.

Above, right:
Studio One Eighty
Nine (brand created
by Rosario Dawson
and Abrima Erwiah),
look from the
spring–summer 2016
collection.
Courtesy of Studio189.

"Afrobougee was first inspired by Tumblr. I could see that the content being posted by African artists was very strong. The art was diverse, and it was different from what you could see in the mainstream. Before Instagram, there were a few brands doing the same thing: the platforms Design Indaba and The African Digital Art, and the Nigerian online magazine *BellaNaija*, but they were never really on the same path as Afrobougee. I created it to spotlight creatives from Africa and to collaborate with them. *Vogue* and other platforms weren't featuring African artists, so we needed a magazine for ourselves. The first slogan was 'Afrobougee for Africans,' then later the platform became a portal for African culture, African creativity, and African art. Today, artists like Lakin Ogunbanwo, Loza Maléombho, and Joana Choumali, or accounts like @everydaypeoplestories by Cedric Nzaka have become stars. When I was younger and working for the Ghana-based magazine *Kenu,* my boss spoke about the Afro community growing and becoming future leaders of their world—the 'new' Africans who were trying to change the narratives, and create new stories and new art. This was very influential for me."

Daron Bandeira
PHOTOGRAPHER AND FOUNDER OF THE PLATFORM @AFROBOUGEE
@daron_bandeira

Facing page:
Photograph
by William Ukoh
(aka Willy Verse)
from the "Lagos
Futurism" series, 2018,
featuring Rebecca
Fabunmi (left)
modeling a jacket by
Maxivive, an outfit
by Orange Culture,
and accessories by
Ladunni Lambo and
Orange Culture;
Eniola Bolarin (center)
modeling a shirt by
Orange Culture, an
aso-oke by I.AM.ISIGO,
a robe by Fruché,
and accessories by
Raya; and Nelson
Oghenekewe (right)
modeling coveralls
by Maxivive, a
neckalce by Raya,
and accessories by
Orange Culture.
Styling: Daniel Obasi.
Makeup: Lauretta Orji.
© Willy Verse (William Ukoh).

Above:
Photograph
by William Ukoh
(aka Willy Verse)
featuring a look from
Loza Maléombho's
spring–summer 2018
collection. Model:
Mah Coulibaly.
© Willy Verse (William Ukoh).

223. Photo

Photograph by
Travys Owen featuring
Manthe, Kokona,
and Tebogo Ribane for
a G-Star advertising
campaign.
© Travys Owen.

FOCUS

"AWOULABA / TAILLE FINE"

BY JOANA CHOUMALI
@joana_choumali

◆

Store mannequins are socio-cultural reflections of their era. In Africa, most of them are imported. High-end stores in Nigeria, South Africa, and Kenya, for example, choose Black mannequins as an obvious means of identification. Elsewhere, notably in small shops in West Africa, white mannequins are still used.

In the 2010s, Ivorian photographer Joana Choumali discovered that in her home city of Abidjan informal manufacturers, working like sculptors, handcraft mannequins from polyester, shaping them according to criteria that better reflect local tastes. The growth of the secondhand and ready-to-wear markets has spurred an enormous increase in demand for these mannequins. On-site production has led to a subtle reconnection with the feminine ideal shared by a large segment of the population, in addition to offering a wider array of skin tones, although not all businesses have adopted the trend. Joana Choumali documents this change "in action" in the series "Awoulaba/Taille Fine" (Awoulaba/Narrow Waist). Awoulaba is the name for "the Queen of Beauty" in Baoulé, one of the languages spoken in Ivory Coast. She has pronounced hips, breasts, and buttocks. There is even a beauty pageant named for her in Ivory Coast, and similar events are held in Senegal, Togo, and Mali, among other countries. These events stand out as acts of resistance in the face of the steamrolling effect of globalization. In contrast, the "narrow waist" corresponds to a Western standard that women have interiorized as a definition of beauty. In this second part of the series, the artist explores the paradoxical demands that weigh on the female body. By superimposing fragments of "real bodies" onto the idealized bodies of women who represent "perfect beauty" in popular culture—Kim Kardashian (the white Awoulaba), Nicki Minaj (the light-skinned Awoulaba), and Naomi Campbell (the narrow-waisted Black woman)—Joana Choumali unpacks the illogical "patchwork" of identity construction that women are forced to engage in. Caught between the ideals of here and elsewhere, the hybrid Venus emerges as the representative of an unrealistic beauty standard.

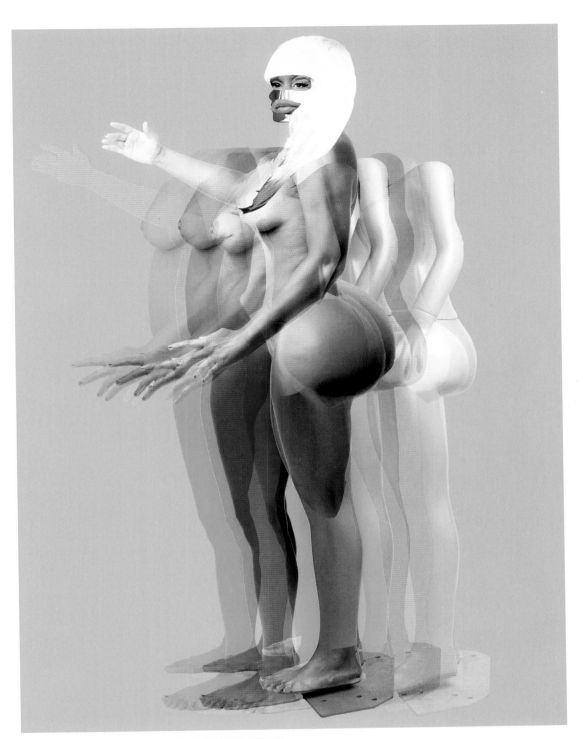

Above:
Digital composite
image juxtaposing
fragments of female
bodies, from the
"Awoulaba/Taille
Fine" series, 2010s.
© Joana Choumali.

Left:
Photographs from
the documentary
series produced
for the "Awoulaba/
Taille Fine" project,
Ivory Coast, 2010s.
© Joana Choumali.

FOCUS

THE SOCIALLY CONSCIOUS SELFIE

"ALIEN EDITS" BY LOZA MALÉOMBHO

@ lozamaleombho

The selfie: one of the great modern myths and the obsession of an entire generation. Africa's youth, like the rest of the world's, is hooked, and has cast itself as the protagonist in a new narrative, a blend of truth and self-(re)construction.

Some call the selfie narcissistic, serving only the ego. In using it to condemn racial, cultural, and religious stereotypes, Ivorian fashion designer Loza Maléombho pushes back against this preconceived idea with irony and a skillful use of mise en abyme. She remembers how she felt "deeply devalued," in her own words, when, in 2014, she heard that the white police officer accused of the murder of young Black man Michael Brown in Ferguson, Missouri, would not be convicted. At the time she was living in both New York and Abidjan in Ivory Coast. While the riots and protests that followed the announcement echoed the violence of racial discrimination suffered by African Americans and the African diaspora, Loza Maléombho began the selfie series "Alien Edits" as a way to cultivate pride and "self-validation"—the exact opposite of those negative sentiments. Drawing on elements particular to traditional and urban African culture, as well as historical figures, the designer shifts the perspective: the Black beauty that she wants to celebrate is, above all, the one she sees around her every day, in Africa. Whether posing with the tall headpiece worn by the eternally fascinating Egyptian queen Nefertiti, "crowned" with a sewing machine—like the one used by the modest tailors found in many African cities—or wearing a ritual mask, Loza Maléombho uses illusion to overturn and reinvent standards of "Beauty." Using chickens, fabric, or tropical flowers, the artist seeks to convey the noble character of an environment often described in condescending terms. Here, the selfie takes on a decidedly socially conscious role. Each subject has an elongated neck that suggests rising above it all and distancing oneself when faced with an affront to one's self-esteem. The artist's hand, present in most of the selfies in the series, takes on a sacramental aspect. Narrative becomes poetry, and resilience—the artist's own—becomes a work of art.

Photographs by Loza
Maléombho from the
"Alien Edits" series
of selfies posted
on Instagram, from
November 5, 2014.
© Loza Maléombho.

Laetitia Ky

ARTIST AND INFLUENCER @laetitiaky

"Like many women, I spent a long time resenting my body for what it is. And careful observation reveals that most of the discrimination we are subjected to relates back to our physical appearance. In my country, some business owners still forbid women to wear natural hairstyles at work. In some ethnic groups, the practice of breast ironing is carried out on girls when they reach puberty: their breasts are flattened to avoid exciting men. I am constantly being whistled at, and if I don't wear a bra under my T-shirt, someone is sure to point it out. People comment on the way I dress, the way I wear my hair; sometimes it borders on harassment. After spending so long wondering 'Why am I like this?' as if I were guilty of something, I wanted to say kind things to my body.

I had been straightening my hair since I was five years old. Then I discovered the ancestral hairstyles worn by African women prior to colonization. They were incredible, like headdresses, sometimes rising high above the head, complete with extensions and braids. When I began to post on Instagram photos of myself wearing these vintage hairstyles, I received an incredible number of messages from women saying that, thanks to me, they were regaining confidence in themselves. It was wild to see just how much people were affected by what I was doing. That's why I continued to place myself at the center of my creations; it's a way of saying that I consider myself to be a work of art as well.

These photos are a message of self-confidence that reaches far beyond what we do with our hair. They are a way of saying, 'Love yourself and take back the power!' I have always been a feminist. My hair sculptures include a series on felines, with the message, 'Be strong and fierce!' There is something within us that frightens men. And even though I constantly come under fire from male critics when I talk about menstruation, abortion, or domestic violence, women must dare to speak out. This is about our bodies and we must take them back."

Pages 232–33: Self-portraits by Laetitia Ky posted on Instagram between 2017 and 2019.
© Laetitia Ky.

Hassan Hajjaj in his
London studio, 2013.
© Jenny Frémont.
Courtesy Hassan Hajjaj.

Hassan Hajjaj

ARTIST @hassanhajjaj_larache

" I grew up without a lot of money, so clothing was a form of self-expression for me and my friends. Then, in my art, it became an extension of this expression, through a very natural and organic process. Some people have pointed to the presence of the veil in the series 'Kesh Angels,' but for me it wasn't about politics or religion—it's about my people, traditions, and culture. Placing logos on traditional outfits not only changes the way people view them, but also generates a feeling of pride and being rooted in where you come from. Through exhibiting my works in different institutions, different countries, and different cultures, I have found that my work raises a lot of debate, especially with regard to how people might perceive my work, but also how it might change (or not) their assumptions about 'Others' and the reality for 'Others.' I witness these debates, because they raise these lines of tension, which are fair. We are all anchored in our culture(s), and sometimes we cannot agree with another culture. I find these debates enriching, when we can agree to disagree, respect one another, and smile together. "

Louis Philippe de Gagoue

PHOTOGRAPHER AND STYLIST
FOUNDER OF *NIKKOU* MAGAZINE @louisphilippedegagoue @nikkoumagazine

"I like mixing genres. To me, there's nothing more poetic. I've lived in Morocco, Tunisia, and Cameroon. I am multicultural, and I've always loved Africa's different heritages, but I am especially a fan of crossing cultures. The hat I'm wearing is a mix between two headdresses: one from the Akan people of Ivory Coast and the other from India. When I began creating images for my blog using myself as the subject, I mixed vintage pieces I found in Tunis with traditional clothes from around the world and items from pop culture. But I also used tajine lids or Canson paper to make peaked hats. I love nothing more than repurposing and being playful, and all the joy that this brings.

I nearly became a lawyer in Nigeria, where the only Bar Association in West Africa is located. I thought I would suffocate under the weight of the black-and-white robe. I need color, which is why I like high-contrast film and bold, sunny hues. That's Africa as I see it and love it.

Nikkou magazine offers a new perspective on my continent. It's about seeing beauty where others don't. It's a courtyard overrun with pigeons, a grocer in a working-class neighborhood, red earth and the sun, that transcendent light. I like playing on the African environment; creating poetic clashes; bringing together luxury and the underground, northern and southern tribes; and finding a balance through clothing. There are no boundaries in my work, but rather singular aesthetics and standpoints that are important to me. It's the same when it comes to beauty: I like Black skin that gleams—that verges on blue, even. I can make it even darker by adjusting the contrasts. It's also a way of showing those who still bleach their skin just how beautiful it is naturally."

© Yasmine Hatimi.

NOTES

INTRODUCTION

1. The Antwerp Six was a group of six designers (including Ann Demeulemeester, Dries Van Noten, and Dirk Bikkembergs), who graduated from the Royal Academy of Fine Arts in Antwerp, Belgium, in the early 1980s. Although their styles differed greatly, they all contributed to designing garments that broke with the codes of mainstream fashion.

2. "Imane Ayissi met la haute-couture à l'heure africaine," *Le Nouvel Observateur*, February 8, 2020.

3. *Africa 2025: What Possible Futures for Sub-Saharan Africa?* (Pretoria: Unisa Press, 2003).

4. Based in Pretoria, South Africa, the African Futures Institute (AFI) is a Pan-African think-tank founded in 2004 by Alioune Sall and specialized in foresight studies.

5. Achille Mbembe, *Black Panther ou le Retournement du Signe Africain* (Paris: Éditions AOC, 2020).

6. Fashion weeks exist in a number of African countries, with some countries hosting several of these events. Dakar Fashion Week (@dakarfashionweek), Lagos Fashion Week (@lagosfashionweekofficial), and South African Fashion Week (@safashionweek) are the most influential on the continent.

7. Nigeria's film industry fluctuates between the second and third largest film industry in the world in terms of annual film production.

8. In Yoruba, one of the languages spoken in Nigeria, *aso* means "fabric" and *ebi* means "family." By extension, *aso-ebi* is a garment worn by all members of an extended family (including friends and even colleagues) during family ceremonies. The codes associated with this "uniform" may include color, fabric, and embroidery.

9. The *gele* is a sophisticated headscarf traditionally worn by Yoruba women. The technique for wrapping it around the face, then knotting it, is a complex art.

10. The term "repat," contrary to "expat" or expatriate, refers to someone who returns to their home country after having lived elsewhere for a significant amount of time.

11. "Third culture kids" are children who are raised in a culture other than their parents' and the culture of their nationality, and who spend significant time in the early years of their development in another environment.

12. Speech delivered on November 30, 2017, in Accra, Ghana, during French president Emmanuel Macron's official visit.

13. Carina Wear (@carina.wear) is a colorful, fashionable brand popular with young Egyptian women.

14. The dashiki tunic, also called Angelina, Miriam Makeba, and Addis Ababa, is a batik tunic created in the 1960s by the Dutch textile company Vlisco.

15. *Africa 2025*.

16. Creator of the blog www.afrosartorialism.net.

17. In response to Alioune Sall's phrase, see note no. 3.

DESIGNERS

TEXTILES, TECHNIQUES, AND INNOVATION

1. *Bazin* is a damask fabric found throughout West Africa, and particularly in Senegal and Mali, from which boubous—long flowing garments worn by men and women alike—are made.

2. Quote by Kenneth Ize taken from an interview with Olivia Singer for vogue.com, October 1, 2020.

3. In July 2016, the renowned Paris concept store hosted a capsule collection by Amine Bendriouich as part of a collaborative project with photographer Hassan Hajjaj.

4. www.amine.bendriouich.com.

5. *Mille Tisserands en Quête d'Avenir* (Bamako: Éditions EDIM, 1999).

INVENTING A LANGUAGE

1. Sunny Dolat and The Nest Collective, *Not African Enough* (Nairobi: Nest Arts Company Limited, 2017).

2. Emmanuelle Courrèges, "Modes africaines," *Something We Africans Got*, no. 5.

3. "Zairianization," or authenticity, was both a policy of nationalizing the economy and reappropriating cultural artifacts that had been abandoned or had disappeared during colonialism. With regards to clothing, the movement encouraged the rejection of the Western suit and tie in favor of the traditional garments or elements of clothing and culture of the former Zaire.

4. Each of these African statesmen displayed their pride in dressing "African" or in garments "made in Africa" at different times and in different countries, and encouraged their populations to do the same.

5. Christopher Burghard Steiner, "Technologies of Resistance: Structural Alteration of Trade Cloth in Four Societies," *Zeitschrift für Ethnologie*, vol. 119, no. 1 (1994): 75–94. Accessed at www.jstor.org/stable/25842347?seq=1.

6. As Joanne B. Eicher explains in her article "A Ping-Pong Example of Cultural Authentication and Kalabari Cut-Thread Cloth," in *Appropriation, Acculturation, Transformation: Textile Society of America 9th Symposium 2004* (Oakland, CA: Textile Society of America, 2005), https://digitalcommons.unl.edu/tsaconf/439: "Although the Kalabari are part of a much larger group of Niger Delta peoples, this cut-thread cloth is original and peculiar to them."

7. According to legend, the Igbo people called this madras "George" in reference to King George of England.

8. This word summarizes a concept of community solidarity among the Igbo people that highlights notions and values of attachment, unity, and "togetherness."

9. The Igbo also call this hat adorned with geometric patterns the Leopard Hat, in reference to secret societies.

10. Isi-agu is a tunic made of cotton or velvet worn by men and printed with lion's heads. It is traditionally worn during Igbo ceremonies in Nigeria.

11. Interview by Emmanuelle Courrèges on lago54.com.

12. Vlisco is a Dutch company that has designed, produced, and distributed wax-print fabrics throughout Africa since 1846.

13. The Mourides are a Sufi Muslim community founded in the late nineteenth century. Their spiritual capital is Touba, Senegal (the city's name appears as an appliqué on one of the dresses in the same collection by Selly Raby Kane). The Mourides play a leading role in Senegalese social, economic, and political life.

14. Interview in an article by Frédéric Joignot, *Le Monde*, February 3, 2011.

15. Created in the eighteenth century, the Asafo are organizations or military companies formed by the Fanti people of Ghana. One of their distinguishing activities is the fabrication of colorful flags that use figures and objects sewn using the appliqué technique to represent elements of political, commercial, and economic life.

16. The Nsibidi is a symbolic method of communication used by the Igbo people in southeast Nigeria. This writing system, made up of ideograms, is a visual vocabulary with thousands of symbols.

17. Alexis Okeowo, "West Africa's Most Daring Designer," *The New Yorker*, September 25, 2017, https://www.newyorker.com/magazine/2017/09/25/the-daring-designs-of-amaka-osakwe.

TALES, HISTORY, AND REBELLIONS

1. Interview with Bubu Ogisi by Emmanuelle Courrèges on lago54.com.

2. *Xibelani* skirts are worn by the VaTsonga women of Mozambique and South Africa, notably during a ritual dance of the same name. These knee-length dresses characterized by several layers of fabric, including two visible, pleated layers, are created from a piece of fabric twenty yards (18 m) long.

3. As the story goes, when Royal Navy captain Frederick E. Forbes (Sarah bears his last name) learned that Sarah's captors were about to sacrifice her, he suggested that King Tsongo offer her to Queen Victoria as a gift.

4. Although legend has it that Sarah Forbes Bonetta was Queen Victoria's goddaughter, her own daughter, named Victoria, became the queen's goddaughter years later. However, a portrait of Sarah Forbes Bonetta hangs in Osborne House, formerly the queen's summer residence.

SUSTAINABLE, ETHICAL, AND ENVIRONMENTALLY RESPONSIBLE FASHION

1. See note no. 13 in "Inventing a Language."

2. *Ndiakhass* means "mixed" in Wolof. Today, this word refers to a patchwork tunic, either handcrafted by the Baye Fall community or manufactured for a more "fashion-focused" use.

3. sellyrabykane.com.

WAX AND AFRICA'S PRINTED FABRICS

1. In the colonial era, what is today Ghana was called the Gold Coast, and the Ashanti people, one of the country's largest ethnic groups, were mobilized to participate in conquests outside of Africa.

2. The Nana Benz were Togolese businesswomen who made their fortune through commercializing and distributing wax-print fabrics, first imported from Togo, then directly from Europe. Some of them became millionaires after signing exclusivity contracts in the 1970s and 1980s; the name "Nana Benz" derives from the Mercedes Benz automobiles they were subsequently able to purchase for themselves.

STYLE

1. Independent researcher and specialist in sustainable fashion in Africa and the African diaspora: www.afrosartorialism.net.

2. The word *sapeur* is derived from SAPE (Société des Ambianceurs et des Personnes Élégantes [Society of Ambiancers and Elegant Persons]), a sartorial movement created in the Democratic Republic of the Congo.

3. In Daniele Tamagni, *Fashion Tribes: Global Street Style* (New York: Abrams, 2015).

4. The L'Boulevard festival was founded in 1999. Lasting three days, it takes place in several cities, each with a specific style of music and events programming: www.boulevard.ma.

5. Amazigh is a language spoken by the Berber people of Morocco.

6. Ga is one of the languages spoken in Ghana.

7. The world's main reserve of coltan—a mineral used in the manufacture of cell phones, computers, and many other electronic products—is found in the Democratic Republic of the Congo, particularly in the Kivu region. The exploitation of these mines is at the heart of a deadly conflict.

8. www.offtomag.com.

9. Laetitia Bouzouita, "Génies créatifs," *Off To*, Kinshasa Issue, 2020.

10. @lartisane.shop.

11. @lesandaga.shop.

12. Pan-Africanism is a doctrine that promotes unity and solidarity between Africans and members of the African diasporas.

13. Kimpa Vita was a seventeenth-century prophetess from the Kongo Kingdom (which at the time reached from today's Republic of the Congo and Democratic Republic of Congo to Angola, and included Gabon), who was burned at the stake by Portuguese colonists.

14. Baoulé weights were once used by the Akan ethnic group in Ghana and Ivory Coast for weighing gold. Today, some stylists or hairdressers use them in their creations.

15. The Tukulor are an ethnic group native to Senegal. In recent years, their *jaaro dibbei* traditional jewelry has experienced a fashion revival, thanks in particular to stylists like Adama Paris.

16. *Isicholo* headdresses are traditionally worn by married Zulu women in South Africa.

17. *Xibelani* skirts are worn by Tsonga women from South Africa during the eponymous traditional dance. This sophisticated skirt, also known as *tinguvu*, is made from several dozen yards of fabric.

18. The *kikoy* (or *kikoi*) is a woven pagne customarily worn as a wrap skirt on the east coast of Africa, particularly in Kenya and Tanzania.

19. *Izimbadada* are traditional Zulu sandals.

20. Alioune Sall (ed.), *Africa 2025: What Possible Futures for Sub-Saharan Africa?* (Pretoria: Unisa Press, 2003).

21. www.baloji.com.

22. Voguing, a highly stylized form of dance that draws inspiration from catwalk poses and ancient Egyptian art, originated in Black and Latino LGBTQ communities in Harlem in the 1960s. It has become fashionable again in recent years.

23. www.noirwave.world.

PHOTO

1. In the 1990s, *Revue Noire* was a prestigious publication that focused on photography, contemporary art, and African critical thought: www.revuenoire.com.

2. https://galerienumber8.com/artists/91-kvvadwo/works.

3. @galerienumber8.

4. @nataalmedia.

5. @oathmagazine.

6. @swag_highprofiles.

7. See note no. II in the introduction.

8. @willyverse.

BIBLIOGRAPHY

BOOKS

ABAZA, Mona. *Changing Consumer Cultures of Modern Egypt: Cairo's Urban Reshaping*. Leiden: Brill, 2006.

ESHUN, Ekow. *Africa 21ème Siècle: Photographie Contemporaine Africaine*. Paris: Textuel, 2020. An exhibition catalog (Rencontres de la Photographie d'Arles, June 29–September 27, 2020).

GROSFILLEY, Anne. *Textiles d'Afrique, entre Tradition et Modernité*. Rouen: Éditions Point de Vues, 2006.

———. *Wax & Co.: Anthologie des Tissus Imprimés d'Afrique*. Paris: Éditions de La Martinière, 2017.

JOUDAR, Hind. *Les Merveilles du Caftan/ The Marvels of the Caftan*. Rabat: Marsam, 2012.

MARIE, Alain. "Introduction: L'Individualisation Africaine en Questions." In *L'Afrique des Individus: Itinéraires Citadins dans l'Afrique Contemporaine (Abidjan, Bamako, Dakar, Niamey)*. Edited by Alain Marie. Paris: Karthala, 2008.

MBEMBE, Achille. *Black Panther ou le Retournement du Signe Africain*. Paris: Éditions AOC, 2020.

McKINLEY, Catherine E. *The African Lookbook: A Visual History of 100 Years of African Women*. New York: Bloomsbury, 2021.

ROVINE, Victoria L. *African Fashion, Global Style: Histories, Innovations, and Ideas You Can Wear*. Bloomington: Indiana University Press, 2015.

SALL, Alioune, ed. *Africa 2025: What Possible Futures for Sub-Saharan Africa?* Pretoria: Unisa, 2003.

SARGENT, Antwaun. *The New Black Vanguard: Photography between Art and Fashion*. New York: Aperture Foundation, 2019.

TAMAGNI, Daniele. *Fashion Tribes: Global Street Style*. New York: Harry N. Abrams, 2015.

TRAORÉ, Aminata Dramane. *Mille Tisserands en Quête de Futur*. Bamako: Éditions EDIM, 1999.

PERIODICALS

ANDRIEU, Bernard, Gilles BOËTSCH, and Dominique CHEVÉ, eds. "Des Corps en Afrique de l'Ouest." *CORPS/Revue Interdisciplinaire*, no.16 (2018).

"La Mode sous Influences: De Diane de Poitiers à Instagram." Special issue, *Revue des Deux Mondes*, 2018.

"Kinshasa Issue." *Off To*, 2020.

Nikkou, no. 3 (2020).

PIVEN, Jean Loup, and N'Goné FALL, eds. "African Fashion." Special issue, *Revue Noire*, no. 27 (December 1997– January/February 1998).

Something We Africans Got, no. 5 (fall 2017).

ARTICLES

AKINWOLE, Tolu. "The Leopard in the Bottle: Language and Characterisation in Chukwuemeka Ike's *The Bottled Leopard*." www.academia.edu.

ARABINDAN-KESSON, Anna. "Presentations of Self: Contemporary African Fashion in a Global World." A book review in *CAA Reviews*, 2012, www.academia.edu.

ASARE, Thomas O., Abdul F. IBRAHIM, and Peggy M. A. HOWARD. "Prospects and Challenges of Smock Industry in Ghana: A Case Study of Tamale Metropolis." *Fashion and Textiles Review*, vol. 1, no. 2 (June 2019).

BARKOVSKI, Valérie. "Mous Lamrabat: A Fashion Photographer." *Darkawa* (blog), November 30, 2019, www.darkawa.net/blog/mous-lamrabat.

CHAHINE, Vicky. "Mode: Des révolutions stylistiques." *Le Point*, May 3, 2020, www.lepoint.fr.

"The Ghanaian Smock: History, Heritage and Pride." *Ghana and Beyond*, October 12, 2019, www.ghanaandbeyond.com.

HASSAN, Zeinab. "Joseph Ouechen photographie la scène punk et métal du Maroc." *Vice*, March 11, 2021, www.vice.com.

HILL, Joseph. "A Mystical Cosmopolitanism: Sufi Hip Hop and the Aesthetics of Islam in Dakar." *Culture and Religion*, vol. 18, no. 4 (2017).

HIRSCH, Valérie. "Une mode pleine de Smarteez." *Libération*, June 4, 2010, www.liberation.fr.

KANE, Selly Raby. Interview with Scheina Adaya. "Je baigne dans l'univers fantastique depuis toute petite." *Intelligences.Info*, April 2, 2021, www.intelligences.info.

LAGARDE, Yann. "L'afro-futurisme, une esthétique de l'émancipation." *France Culture*, September 6, 2019, www.franceculture.fr.

MAITLAND, Hayley. "26-Year-Old Photographer Nadine Ijewere on Her Historic *Vogue* Cover." *Vogue*, December 12, 2018, www.vogue.com.

MZOUGHI, Jihen. "Born between Two, Abdel El Tayeb Built a Nation of His Own." *Mille*, February 1, 2021, www.milleworld.com.

PHILLIPS, Lior. "Baloji's Vibrant New Video Looks at Congolese Pygmy Wedding Traditions." *Dazed*, March 22, 2018, www.dazeddigital.com.

PICARELLI Enrica. "Selly Raby Kane: Surrealist Designer and Social Innovator." *Fashion Studies*, vol. 2, no. 1 (2019).

ROVINE, Victoria L. "Mode africaine: Réseaux mondiaux et styles locaux." *Africultures*, no. 69 (2006).

TOURÉ, Katia. "Ibaaku: 'L'afro-futurisme, c'est l'Afrique moderne qui se tourne vers elle-même.'" *Le Point*, February 19, 2017, www.lepoint.fr.

VALENTIN, Anne-Sophie. "Comment Guy Bourdin a révolutionné la photographie de mode." *Les Inrockuptibles*, April 4, 2016, www.lesinrocks.com.

ACKNOWLEDGMENTS

I am extremely grateful to all those, both near and far, who contributed their knowledge to this book, made fruitful connections possible, and generously shared their time.

First of all, I wish to thank my parents for my wandering feet and my Southern heart, and for their love and unwavering support, which was invaluable during the writing process.

I also extend my thanks to my dear sisters, Sika, Sarah, and Awa L. who, during this period of research and writing marked by the Covid pandemic, were particularly generous with their presence and affection.

A special thank-you goes to my friend Jean-Marc Chauve, fashion historian and professor at the Institut Français de la Mode, whose attention, advice, feedback, and support were fundamental.

I wish to express my particular thanks to the following people:

Alioune Sall, director of the African Futures Institute (IFA/Pretoria)

Simon Njami, author and curator

Amadou Diaw, founder of the Forum de Saint-Louis (forumdesaintlouis.org)

Giordano Tamagni

Leanne Tlhagoane

Enrica Picarelli, independent researcher and media consultant specializing in sustainability and fashion in Africa and its diaspora (www.afrosartorialism.net)

Jeanne Mercier, cofounder of Afrique in Visu, a platform for photographers in Africa (www.afriqueinvisu.org)

Aminata Dramane Traoré, sociologist and writer

Gilles Boëtsch, anthropologist and director of research emeritus at the CNRS

Victoria Rovine, art historian specializing in sartorial practices and African textiles, Adjunct Faculty, Department of African, African American, and Diaspora Studies, University of North Carolina

Mona Abaza, professor of sociology, Department of Sociology, Egyptology, and Anthropology, American University in Cairo

Cyrus Dennis, Afropunk (afropunk.com)

Sharon Cooper-Quann, Afropunk, Johannesburg

Papama Mtwisha, founder of Africa Your Time Is Now (www.africayourtimeisnow.com/our-story)

Mamy Tall, architect and cofounder of @Dakarlives

Daron Bandeira, photographer (@daron_bandeira)

Emmanuel Ekuban, editor-in-chief of @debonairafrik, @nuelbans

Bréhima Guindo, Centre Amadou Hampathé Bâ, Bamako

Dr. Aka Konin, general director of the Ivory Coast Cultural Heritage Office

Hilaire Kwassy Kra, Ivory Coast Cultural Heritage Office

Duncan Clarke, specialist in Yoruba woven cloth and founder of Adire African Textiles, a website for traditional African textiles (www.adireafricantextiles.com)

Annette Pringle, The Fashion Agent (@thefashionagent)

Lina Ibrahim, artist and costume designer (www.linakhalil.com, @lina_aly)

Florence Quentin, Egyptologist

Hind Joudar, journalist and founder of the Oriental Fashion Show (orientalfashionshow.com)

Marie Gomis-Trezise, creative director of Nataal Media; founder and curator of Galerie Number 8 (www.nataal.com, @nataalmedia, www.galerienumber8.com)

Helen Jennings, editorial director of Nataal (www.nataal.com, @nataalmedia)

Jo Evendon, photo editor and producer at Dazed magazine

Erica de Greef, cofounder of the African Fashion Research Institute (@afri_digital, afri.digital/african-fashion-why-do-these-stereotypes-exist-and-persist/)

Marie-Jeanne Serbin Thomas, director of Brune magazine

Stéphanie Simon, Nikkou magazine

Louise Ramspacher, Nikkou magazine

Déborah Benzaquen, photographer

Faridah Folawiyo

Laetitia Dechanet, deputy editor of Diptyk Magazine – L'Art Vu du Maroc

Finally, this book would not exist without the bold vision of Julie Rouart, editorial director of the Art department at Flammarion. I thank her warmly for the trust she placed in me. I would also like to thank my editor, Gaëlle Lassée, for her patience; picture researcher Marie-Catherine Audet, for her courage in carrying out a Herculean task; Séléna Richez and Yaël Rusé, for their valuable assistance to us all; designer Mateo Baronnet, for his remarkable creativity in giving form to the "fashion continent"; and Kate Mascaro and Helen Adedotun, for their work on the English-language edition. And last but not least, I express my sincere gratitude to Béatrice Mocquard, who was at the origin of this project.

French Edition

Editorial Director
Julie Rouart

Administration Manager
Delphine Montagne

Literary Director
Gaëlle Lassée
assisted by **Séléna Richez** and **Yaël Rusé**

Image Selection
Emmanuelle Courrèges

Picture Research
Marie-Catherine Audet

Design and Typesetting
Studio B49 _ Mateo Baronnet

English Edition

Editorial Director
Kate Mascaro

Editor
Helen Adedotun

Translation from the French
Kate Robinson

Copyediting
Lindsay Porter

Proofreading
Sarah Kane

Production
Corinne Trovarelli

Color Separation
Quadrilaser

Printed in Portugal by **Printer Portuguesa**

Simultaneously published in French as
Swinging Africa: Le Continent Mode
© Flammarion, S.A., Paris, 2021

English-language edition
© Flammarion, S.A., Paris, 2021

21 22 23 3 2 1
ISBN: 978-2-08-151341-9
Legal Deposit: 11/2021

The Publisher has made every effort to
identify the rights holders of the images
reproduced in this book. Any errors or
omissions are inadvertent and will be
corrected in subsequent printings upon
notification.